DECADE

Twenty new plays about 9/11 and its legacy

Samuel Adamson ■ Mike Bartlett ■ Alecky Blythe

Adam Brace ■ Ben Ellis ■ Ella Hickson ■ Samuel D. Hunter

John Logan ■ Matthew Lopez ■ Mona Mansour ■ DC Moore

Abi Morgan ■ Rory Mullarkey ■ Janine Nabers

Lynn Nottage ■ Harrison David Rivers ■ Simon Schama

Christopher Shinn ■ Beth Steel ■ Alexandra Wood

NICK HERN BOOKS
London
www.nickhernbooks.co.uk

A Nick Hern Book

Decade first published in Great Britain in 2011 as a paperback original by Nick Hern Books Limited, 14 Larden Road, London W3 7ST, in association with Headlong

Cover designed by Ned Hoste, 2H
Cover image by feastcreative.com

Typeset by Nick Hern Books, London
Printed and bound in Great Britain by CPI Group (UK) Ltd, Croydon, CR0 4YY

A CIP catalogue record for this book is available from the British Library

ISBN 978 1 84842 230 8

Other Titles in this Series

Howard Brenton
ANNE BOLEYN
BERLIN BERTIE
FAUST – PARTS ONE & TWO *after* Goethe
IN EXTREMIS
NEVER SO GOOD
PAUL
THE RAGGED TROUSERED
    PHILANTHROPISTS *after* Tressell

Alecky Blythe
CRUISING
THE GIRLFRIEND EXPERIENCE
LONDON ROAD

Jez Butterworth
JERUSALEM
JEZ BUTTERWORTH PLAYS: ONE
MOJO
THE NIGHT HERON
PARLOUR SONG
THE WINTERLING

Caryl Churchill
BLUE HEART
CHURCHILL PLAYS: THREE
CHURCHILL PLAYS: FOUR
CHURCHILL: SHORTS
CLOUD NINE
A DREAM PLAY *after* Strindberg
DRUNK ENOUGH TO SAY
    I LOVE YOU?
FAR AWAY
HOTEL
ICECREAM
LIGHT SHINING IN
    BUCKINGHAMSHIRE
MAD FOREST
A NUMBER
SEVEN JEWISH CHILDREN
THE SKRIKER
THIS IS A CHAIR
THYESTES *after* Seneca
TRAPS

Ariel Dorfman
DEATH AND THE MAIDEN
PURGATORIO
READER
THE RESISTANCE TRILOGY
WIDOWS

Stella Feehily
BANG BANG BANG
DREAMS OF VIOLENCE
DUCK
O GO MY MAN

Debbie Tucker Green
BORN BAD
DIRTY BUTTERFLY
RANDOM
STONING MARY
TRADE & GENERATIONS
TRUTH AND RECONCILIATION

Ella Hickson
EIGHT
HOT MESS &
    PRECIOUS LITTLE TALENT

Sam Holcroft
COCKROACH
DANCING BEARS
PINK
WHILE YOU LIE

Lucy Kirkwood
BEAUTY AND THE BEAST
    with Katie Mitchell
BLOODY WIMMIN
HEDDA *after* Ibsen
IT FELT EMPTY WHEN THE HEART
    WENT AT FIRST BUT
    IT IS ALRIGHT NOW
TINDERBOX

Conor McPherson
DUBLIN CAROL
McPHERSON PLAYS: ONE
McPHERSON PLAYS: TWO
PORT AUTHORITY
THE SEAFARER
SHINING CITY
THE VEIL
THE WEIR

DC Moore
THE SWAN

Chloë Moss
CHRISTMAS IS MILES AWAY
FATAL LIGHT
HOW LOVE IS SPELT
THE WAY HOME
THIS WIDE NIGHT

Bruce Norris
CLYBOURNE PARK
THE PAIN AND THE ITCH

Lynn Nottage
RUINED

Jack Thorne
2ND MAY 1997
BUNNY
STACY & FANNY AND FAGGOT
WHEN YOU CURE ME

Enda Walsh
BEDBOUND & MISTERMAN
DELIRIUM
DISCO PIGS & SUCKING DUBLIN
ENDA WALSH PLAYS: ONE
THE NEW ELECTRIC BALLROOM
THE SMALL THINGS
THE WALWORTH FARCE

Alexandra Wood
THE ELEVENTH CAPITAL
UNBROKEN

Contents

Foreword

Rupert Goold and Robert Icke

Headlong makes big new plays about provocative, contemporary subjects. Having looked at the financial crisis and at climate change, in mid-2010 we began talking about 9/11 on its tenth anniversary. There will be people who rehearse the argument that theatre has no valid role in examining recent trauma and disaster, but – while it's certainly true that bad art about any tragedy could be offensive – we have no doubt that theatre is at its most urgent and essential when asking questions about the things that most disturb and frighten us. And, as was later verified on both sides of the Atlantic, 9/11 proved to be an issue that people were burning either to avoid or to talk about. Either way, it felt like there was something to explore.

It was early in the development of *Decade* that we decided it needed to be a multi-writer production. Everyone can tell you where they were that day. And everyone has a different opinion about 9/11 and its legacies. Combine this with our desire for the piece to have a broader viewpoint than just that of London or New York, and a wilfully fragmented form seemed essential – a Babel with no claims to neatness, where different voices, political viewpoints and forms would fight it out. The progression of the show would come through contraries, not through unity; and the piece itself would endorse no particular political agenda.

We started conversations with several writers we were excited by, asking simply for a piece responding to 9/11 or its legacies, lasting between thirty seconds and fifteen minutes. And, as well as reading a large number of pitches which came in for the project, we set up two development workshops – one in London and one in New York – which were, it turned out, where the show really started to crystallise. Each workshop was attended by a hand-picked group of ten to twelve exciting, emerging writers, and each had the same structure: an evening of group discussion and exercises followed by a weekend of writing punctuated by dramaturgical consultations based on the few pages or whole scripts written thus far.

Just outside London, heated discussions went on into the early hours
– and at The Public Theater in New York, on a weekend which was
to end with the death of Bin Laden, writers talked with humour and
passion about 9/11's various aftermaths in the last decade. And,
though we could never have hoped to include all of the work
created, even in a three-hour show, these workshops marked the
moment where we saw – with some excitement – the production
itself first begin to emerge.

This is not a playscript of the production we will create (at the time
of publication, the shape of the show is changing daily) but a
collection of the material we rehearsed and developed in the
rehearsal room. There isn't space in this foreword to tell the full
story of our inspirations in creating this production, or our process in
developing it, but as a company dedicated to ambitious and
provocative new plays, we are proud and excited to be making a
piece of work which is already inspiring opposing and passionate
reactions – and which has produced this extraordinary collection of
plays.

Headlong
September 2011

Headlong
DECADE

Writers
Samuel Adamson
Mike Bartlett
Alecky Blythe
Adam Brace
Ben Ellis
Ella Hickson
Samuel D. Hunter
John Logan
Matthew Lopez
Mona Mansour
DC Moore
Abi Morgan
Rory Mullarkey
Janine Nabers
Lynn Nottage
Harrison David Rivers
Simon Schama
Christopher Shinn
Beth Steel
Alexandra Wood

Ensemble Cast (in alphabetical order)
Jonathan Bonnici
Leila Crerar
Emma Fielding
Kevin Harvey
Tom Hodgkins
Samuel James
Arinze Kene
Amy Lennox
Tobias Menzies
Claire Prempeh
Charlotte Randle
Cat Simmons

Chloe Faty
Isabella Mason
Charlotte St Croix

Creative Team
Director: Rupert Goold
Set Designer: Miriam Buether
Costume Designer: Emma Williams
Choreographer: Scott Ambler
Lighting Designer: Malcolm Rippeth
Composer & Sound Designer: Adam Cork
Associate Director: Robert Icke
Assistant Director: Nadia Latif
Technical Sound Design: Sebastian Frost
Casting: Pippa Ailion

Decade was conceived and developed by Rupert Goold
with Robert Icke.

With thanks to The Public Theater, New York.

Decade is the result of Headlong's collaboration with many
writers.

Decade is produced in association with Chichester Festival
Theatre.

First performance of *Decade* at Commodity Quay, St Katharine
Docks, London, on 1 September 2011.

www.headlongtheatre.co.uk

Headlong

Headlong makes exhilarating, provocative and spectacular new work to take around the country and around the world.

Headlong is one of the UK's leading theatre companies. Led by award-winning Artistic Director Rupert Goold, Headlong is dedicated to new ways of making theatre. We collaborate with the most exciting and adventurous theatre artists in the country and provide them with the time, resources and creative support to allow them to make their most challenging work.

We are interested in theatre that asks provocative questions of the world we live in today in the most vibrant and theatrical forms we can imagine. The focus of our work is new writing but we also look to develop new and emerging artists through dynamic and ambitious revivals. We run workshops and placement programmes for the writers, directors, designers and producers of the future; practitioners who have emerged under Headlong's support are now some of the leading theatre artists around the world.

'Wild, mad and deeply intelligent theatre'

Sunday Times

Headlong Theatre is:

Rupert Goold	Artistic Director
Henny Finch	Executive Producer
Jenni Kershaw	Executive Producer (Maternity Cover)
Robert Icke	Associate Director
Julie Renwick	Finance Manager
Lindsey Alvis	Assistant Producer
Louisa Norman	Assistant Producer
Jamie Lloyd	Associate Artist

'Rupert Goold is the finest director of his generation'

Evening Standard

Supported by
ARTS COUNCIL ENGLAND

www.headlongtheatre.co.uk

RECOLLECTIONS OF SCOTT FORBES

Edited by Samuel Adamson

Characters

SCOTT FORBES, *fifty in 2011, born Widness, lives London,
    resident New York City 1998–2003*

My brain tells me there's no danger.

This plane's full of water to put out the flames on the first tower, like a forest fire. So I just watch it, and watch it, and watch it; and then it comes over to fifteen degrees to my right, and the wings dip and it goes what I think – what my brain tells me – is behind the Towers; so I'm confused because I thought it was going to drop water on it; and then it doesn't come from the side, so I'm like, where's it gone? Because I'm on the west, so I can't see anything, the Towers are hiding me from what's going on; what I'm seeing from my living room, I don't see on TV, what I'm seeing on TV shows me flames, and the plane going into the building, so, um, I'm swearing down the phone to Bernard and then...

then our building is transformed into sand.

It goes like this, (*Demonstrates.*) this sandcastle falling down.

And Bernard and I, both of us were like,

— 'This is complete madness, what's going on?'

and both of us kind of at the same time say,

— 'What did we do at the weekend? What the hell did I do at the weekend?'

I felt almost responsible. I felt like it was something we'd done on our technical systems that caused the building to collapse. I felt guilty.

* * *

The best was that you'd be looking over the clouds. Sometimes, you'd be above them so you couldn't see anything; you were just above the clouds with planes flying around you. My company was on five floors in the South Tower; I worked on the ninety-seventh. Our cafeteria faced north – and I can show you a picture – the view was *that*, towards the Empire State; so you'd be looking all the way up Manhattan, and if you're sitting there having breakfast and that's your view, it takes your breath away, particularly when you see a plane flying across; or on 9/11 – I didn't see it because I wasn't there – one of my colleagues saw the plane coming down and hitting the other tower, from the cafeteria.

You never got bored, every day was different. There was always something going on. It was like being in a cinema, with screens all around you.

I loved the World Trade Center. I did, I loved it. It was a glory to work in.

* * *

I lived as the crow flies a mile and a half from the Trade Center, across the Hudson, in Jersey City; I looked straight at it from my living room. At night it would be lit up, and in the morning, the sun would be rising behind it. I found it astonishing to look at. It would change colour, depending on the light and clouds. Every day was different. It just kind of reflected everything that was going on around it. It was a very proud piece of Manhattan. I remember once one of my colleagues, Mark, said,

— 'I hate the Trade Center,'

and I was really angry with him,

— 'How can you say that, this is such a symbol for New York and America; look how beautiful that façade is, it's absolutely beautiful!'

I think he was reflecting about how he didn't like his job; I was talking architecturally about this structure, which wasn't just a structure; it embodied a city, it embodied a time, it embodied a country, and I was proud of it; and just to take that thought on a bit, on 9/11, when the first plane hit and there were flames and so on – I remember I felt really guilty about having this thought at the time – I felt that the symmetry was broken, and I was more angry about that than anything, and that's a terrible thing to say, really, but I was really upset about that. 'Well, if that Tower's been on fire, companies are not going to be in, so it's all going to be black and horrible, but we're going to work in the Tower, and it's probably going to be two weeks and it's going to be temporary offices, oh, bloody hell.' Instinctive and initial: 'Oh, crap, I'm going to work in a building with one Tower.'

It's difficult to explain. Probably I've not fully realised how important the building was to me.

It was... a bit like an altar. It was... absolutely... um... dominant.

* * *

The day before 9/11, we went to a Mexican restaurant for lunch and had frozen cocktails because my manager Rod was pissed off and he was like,

— 'I don't care, we're going out.'

Three weeks earlier, the company had been given notice by the Port Authority that the power supply on the top fifty per cent of the South Tower would be halted for a period on the 8th and 9th of September, for a re-cabling exercise. As a financial institution we were required to have recoverable systems, so on Saturday the 8th we had to power things down logically – applications, databases, the network, hardware – lots of ancillary pieces as well, like external connections and feeds, all sorts of stuff, it was very complicated; you know, this is why I remember it so vividly. Once all of our systems were down, we handed the environment over to the Port Authority. Just over twenty-four hours later, on Sunday the 9th, we were told, 'Okay, the power's back, you can start everything up again.' Now the vast majority of systems came back up fine. But two were a problem, and on Monday the 10th we just couldn't get one of them up and running and my manager Rod just made the decision – he was like that – so four of us went to this Mexican place. I drank like a great big yellow thing, and when we went back to the office we were all, 'whey-hey'; that afternoon, we were in a really good mood.

At seven, I took the ferry home. I'd arranged to take the 11th off with another guy who normally took Tuesdays off. That was Carlos. As I left, Bernard said,

— 'See you tomorrow, Scott.'

— 'No you won't; I've got the day off, I need a break, 'cause I worked at the weekend,'

and Bernard was jealous so he arranged to take the day off as well.

And I don't know if it's my imagination, but I can remember sitting on top of the ferry – lovely, lovely evening – wistfully watching the Trade Center going off in the distance.

It was nice. It was warm. And then, a very quiet night.

* * *

It sounded like a big juggernaut jumping in the road like it hit a block. I went to the window and looked down and there was nothing. Then I looked up, and I remember it was a Spielberg moment, it was that *boom-boom-boom*, that focus in my eyes just went onto it: smoke rising from the North Tower. I thought it was coming out of the Windows on the World restaurant and I just kind of looked at it for three or four seconds and instinctively felt really bad about it and picked up my phone and dialled the first number I could think of in the office which was Mark. He answered immediately on speakerphone,

— 'Did you hear that?'

— 'Yes, Mark, I heard it, but there's smoke coming out of the North Tower, I feel really bad about this,'

— 'Was there an explosion or something?'

— 'I don't know, Mark, but it looks really bad, I feel really bad about it,'

— 'Okay, okay, I think we're going to evacuate.'

— 'Okay.'

I knew he wouldn't move. Mark sat in the same cubicle as I; like this; I'm here, he was there. He would come in and sit there in the morning for half an hour and do nothing, it used to irritate me beyond belief because he would take his shoes off, he would put his soft shoes on, he would get a tissue, he'd move his coffee around, he would turn his bloody machine; really annoyed me, so I knew he would faff around and be taking his soft shoes off and putting his hard shoes on, he'd be gathering his bag together, he'd have to get his Filofax, so I just hit redial,

— 'What?'

— 'Mark, you've got to get out, I feel really bad about this!'

— 'Okay, okay,'

and at the same time another colleague, Brian, shouted,

— 'Is that Scott? Was it a plane?'

— 'I don't know, hold on,'

and I turned on the TV and they showed a picture from the north, so I'm looking from the west eastwards and I'm seeing pictures from the north, so I say to Mark,

— 'They're saying a plane has hit the Tower, I think they think it's a passenger jet,'

— 'Holy shit, we're going.'

* * *

I didn't hear from Mark until midnight. He got out. He spoke to Rod, my boss; he spoke to his boss, Ed; to a few other people:

— 'We've gotta go, we've gotta go,'

and none of them would go, so Mark left with another colleague. He was lucky.

Carlos sat next to Mark on the other side of the cubicle. He heard our conversation, he also heard the plane hit, and he didn't speak to anyone, he just picked up his bag and walked out, great instinct. He just got out, no small talk, nothing, just left. Of course I was concerned because I'd swapped time off with him.

Brian didn't get out. Brian was killed.

Rod my boss was killed.

Ed, Mark's boss, was killed.

All of our managers in Technology were killed, none of them were left.

* * *

It took me a while to start thinking the powerdown through. After about six months, I got in touch with the 9/11 Commission and the Port Authority to get a full explanation. I didn't get any response from either of them.

In 2003 I said something really naive on a blog like,

— 'Hello, my name is Scott Forbes, I worked in the Trade Center on 9/8 and 9/9; there was a powerdown; I've not been able to register this with the 9/11 Commission, I'm not able to get any further information, can anyone help me find out more and duh-duh-duh' –

and I was *inundated* with responses, I got *hundreds* of emails, some of them quite bizarre; some of them, terrifying. One was some guy asking me if I was

— 'The Scott Forbes that had an IBM laptop with the chip number so-and-so purchased in 1992?'

and the answer is yes! Where the hell did he get that information from? I had one guy in Sri Lanka telling me,

— 'You are an American patriot!'

and I politely told him,

— 'I'm no such thing, how dare you?'

(*Laughs*.) I was contacted by journalists and radio stations and TV stations and the guy who made *Loose Change*, this film about the US government being responsible for 9/11. It's a fascinating film; a high-level conspiracy story with a contemporary soundtrack; it's like a piece of inner-city cinematic hiphop; a great piece of amateur, online editing that fed on and into the 9/11 Truth phenomenon. When he spoke to me, he already had the first version on YouTube and going viral. I explained about my day off and the powerdown, but when I cautioned I was still working for the company and couldn't use the company name, he dropped me like a lead balloon.

Frankly I'm not sure I was sensational enough.

You know, 9/11 occurred in parallel with the growth and power of online media, and in a way I regretted making that blog entry because it was like, 'Oh, I've released this demon now, this is quite scary.' Some of the stuff I've had to deal with is ludicrous. I was invited to a 9/11 group meeting in the House of Commons. After, there was a guy asking me questions about disaster recovery procedures; he does the same job as me and he was testing whether I was genuine or not. And I felt elated: this is validation, you know? The next person that comes to me gives me a CD with his theories on it that

— 'Invisible spacecraft were sending power beacons against the Trade Center to demolish it,'

and it's like: where do these people come from? I had one woman who pestered me and has sent me endless emails because she wants to

— 'Paint your aura.'

(*Laughs.*) And it's like,

— 'Okay, I've got an aura, but I'm not interested, love.'

I'm trying to make a serious point: the 9/11 Truth movement is like a magnet for these disparate people, and a lot aren't there for the truth, they've got their own truth already. I've been labelled by these people, and if you don't fulfil what they see as an obligation, they're not happy. They're as political as any politician: they're happy to use you when it suits and not when it doesn't.

* * *

I'm not a conspiracy theorist. I don't have a theory, that's wrong. Some accuse me of being a 9/11 Truther and of having an agenda: I don't have an agenda. Some have said I don't work for the company, and I do. Never did work for the company: and I did, I do. Some have told me I'm lying. And I'm not. Some want me to be, um, like, a hero? And I don't want to be a hero, I just want the truth.

You know, the building came down on 9/11. Two days before, we had a powerdown when electric cabling was removed and replaced. I saw contractors. I saw workmen in overalls with boxes and cables on the lobby of the seventy-sixth floor. It did occur, and I want it explained. I want to know the contracting company or companies that were there and I want to know how many people, and I'd like to know exactly what they were doing. I'm sure in the Port Authority there are records. Conceivably access to those building spaces... could have been a risk... it could have been... you know... if I... putting it out there blindly... I don't say I believe this, but... these outrageous ideas that are there... I'm not saying I believe, but –

— I met this guy, William Rodriguez, who escaped as the building collapsed. He was a janitor, worked for the Port Authority: he's called the Last Man Out. He was hailed as a hero by the American media and given a presidential medal of honour because he saved people; he had keys to open doors that were locked and so on. His testimony is incredible. Apparently, there was a delivery guy delivering sodas; the van had driven down, and he was delivering these soft drinks four floors underground, and Rodriguez went down and rescued him from the rubble.

Rodriguez was called to the 9/11 Commission, and he says there were explosions in the basement of the World Trade Center. The guy he rescued validates the story.

None of this was included in the report. He asked for it to be made public, though it never was; it was held in private session, and it was never acknowledged or published.

He was dropped by the media and politicians. So, you know, because his story doesn't fit the official storyline, he becomes invisible: except he doesn't. He's all over the web. He goes around the world giving this lecture. He's become incredibly well-known. He's one of the very few 9/11 Truth celebrities, if you like.

Kind of interesting.

* * *

It seems virtually impossible, at the moment, with my information, to get proof, to get concrete evidence. I can't get the information out there which nobody can deny that this powerdown occurred. Uh... it's really... I can't get it... I can't do it. The fact that the 9/11 Commission in particular didn't acknowledge my information or didn't deem it to be important upset me, because all information is important. It just leaves a gaping hole; even more so after reading about how inefficient and unfocused they were, how clearly they were given a remit by the White House on what they could look at and not look at, on what they could say and not say.

You know, that's where all my questioning and anxiety arose from.

It's just disappointment all round.

I do honestly want to get to the bottom of it.

Hopefully one day I will.

* * *

I don't want to sound cynical, but I'm not optimistic about the world. I don't mean that with a heavy heart, it's just the way it is; you know, that's what experience teaches you. You can find your optimism wherever – in a flower, or an uninterrupted journey home – but on that political level you can't really talk about optimism, and if somebody does, they're not being genuine; it's Disney. This has been a decade politically of cynicism; people are very cynical of cause and effect now in politics. Political decisions were made which have piggybacked on 9/11. Individual politicians made of it what they will, and still do. Like Bush and Blair and Giuliani. Regarding Bush now I have... um... (*Laughs.*) it's funny... I don't feel... you know, he's almost like a vacuum. (*Laughs.*) Blair on the other hand is very not a vacuum. Blair used 9/11. Eulogised about it. Put a lot of weight on it. Used it to validate his support of Iraq. I think Blair is pivotal, Bush isn't. You know he was called to the Iraq Inquiry and he was so over-prepared for that. There's no simple honesty there: and no, that is *not* endemic to politicians; I think it's a weakness of *some* politicians, some very able politicians.

There were nearly a hundred Brits on 9/11. And there was a memorial put up to them in New York. And there are events regularly supported by the British Embassy and Blair – along with lots of other bodies, charitable foundations and so on – and that's the irony; you know, on 9/11 I should have been in the office, but I took the day off, and I would have been in the office when the plane hit, I wouldn't have left. Had I died on 9/11, I would have been one of the people honoured by Blair: now I'm a survivor but I'm not.

I feel powerless in relation to 9/11, really powerless.

It's like purgatory.

THE ENEMY

Mike Bartlett

14

Characters

JOHN

MAN

Note on the Text

(/) means the next speech begins at that point.
(–) means the next line interrupts.
(…) at the end of a speech means it trails off. On its own it indicates a pressure, expectation or desire to speak.

A speech with no written dialogue indicates a character deliberately remaining silent.

Blank space between speeches in the dialogue indicates a silence equal to the length of the space.

JOHN *is waiting. The* MAN *approaches him.*

JOHN	Hi
MAN	Hi
JOHN	Okay.
MAN	What?
JOHN	No no. So you're the…
MAN	What?
JOHN	You're the one who…
MAN	What?
JOHN	It's just –
MAN	Okay.
JOHN	I'm John.
MAN	Right.
JOHN	They said –
MAN	Can I?
JOHN	Yeah.
MAN	Thanks.
JOHN	They said –
MAN	What?
JOHN	Wait here.
MAN	Okay.
JOHN	Stay here and he'll find you.
MAN	Right.
JOHN	He'll find you.
MAN	Yeah.

JOHN	So you're –
MAN	Yeah.
JOHN	Him?
MAN	Yeah.
JOHN	Okay
MAN	Okay
JOHN	So what's your –
MAN	What?
JOHN	Your –
MAN	I can't –
JOHN	Your name
MAN	I can't tell you.
JOHN	Of course.
MAN	Of course not.
JOHN	But you're –
MAN	Yeah
JOHN	The one who –
MAN	Yeah.
JOHN	Okay.
	Okay.
MAN	So what?
JOHN	No.
MAN	What now?
JOHN	I've got
MAN	Cos I –
JOHN	I've got
MAN	Other places.

JOHN	No I'm just
MAN	Okay
JOHN	Nervous.
MAN	Why?
JOHN	Why am I –
MAN	Nervous. Why would you be –
JOHN	Be nervous?
MAN	Yeah.
JOHN	Well –
MAN	What?
JOHN	It's a big –
MAN	What?
JOHN	You.
MAN	What?
JOHN	You're –
MAN	What?
JOHN	Him.
MAN	Just a job.
JOHN	I know but –
MAN	Trained.
JOHN	Come on.
MAN	What?
JOHN	You must
MAN	What?
JOHN	Feel it.
MAN	What?
JOHN	Pride.
MAN	No

JOHN	No pride?
MAN	No.
JOHN	Joy.
MAN	Joy?
JOHN	Anger.
MAN	Control.
JOHN	Did you –
MAN	What?
JOHN	Have any –
MAN	Have any?
JOHN	Know any –
MAN	What?
JOHN	Anyone who –
MAN	What?
JOHN	Died.
MAN	Of course.
JOHN	No. But –
MAN	Jesus.
JOHN	On that.
MAN	What?
JOHN	That day.
MAN	Oh.
JOHN	In the –
MAN	The Towers.
JOHN	The Pentagon?
MAN	Yeah.
JOHN	Either.
MAN	Yeah.

JOHN   You did?

MAN   Yeah.

JOHN   Who?

MAN   …

JOHN   Who?

MAN   What?

JOHN   Who was –

MAN   You want…

JOHN   What was –

MAN   A name?

JOHN   No who was he?

MAN   He?

JOHN   Your

MAN   What?

JOHN   Who died.

MAN   She

JOHN   She?

MAN   Yeah.

JOHN   Okay.

MAN   Yeah.

JOHN   What was *she*?

MAN   I don't.

JOHN   To you.

MAN   No.

JOHN   To you I mean.

MAN   She was –

JOHN   A friend?

MAN   I don't.

JOHN	You knew her
MAN	She was good.
JOHN	A good –
MAN	Yeah.
JOHN	A good friend?
MAN	Good girl.
JOHN	Good girl.
MAN	Yeah.

JOHN	And you.
	You knew her from.
	From…
	What?
	School?
MAN	No
JOHN	College
MAN	No.
JOHN	What?
MAN	Why?
JOHN	Just a
MAN	Yeah.
JOHN	A friend.
MAN	Yeah.
JOHN	Not a
MAN	No.
JOHN	You and
MAN	No.
JOHN	Her.

MAN	No.
JOHN	You didn't.
MAN	No.
JOHN	Ever.
MAN	Not your
JOHN	Close?
MAN	Business.
JOHN	You were –
MAN	Sarah
JOHN	Okay.
MAN	That's –
JOHN	That's her name.
MAN	Yeah
JOHN	Yeah.
MAN	Pentagon.
JOHN	Okay.
MAN	Yeah.
JOHN	She worked –
MAN	She worked in the –
JOHN	Yeah. There.
MAN	There.
JOHN	Yeah.
MAN	Okay.
JOHN	Yeah.
	You didn't...
MAN	What?
JOHN	Did you ever...

MAN	No.
JOHN	You and.
MAN	No.
JOHN	Her?
MAN	Stop.
JOHN	Cos they'll
MAN	What?
JOHN	Want to know.
MAN	Who?
JOHN	Readers.
MAN	Why?
JOHN	Human.
MAN	What?
JOHN	This is
MAN	Human?
JOHN	All about the
MAN	No.
JOHN	Human side
MAN	Human side
JOHN	All about –
MAN	*What?*
JOHN	You.
MAN	No.
JOHN	So this.
MAN	Not what I
JOHN	Her.
MAN	No.
JOHN	*Sarah.*

MAN	No.
JOHN	You loved
MAN	Not the
JOHN	Loved her?
MAN	Not the story.
JOHN	It is.
MAN	The mission.
JOHN	No.
MAN	That's the
JOHN	No.
MAN	Story.
JOHN	I say.
MAN	What?
JOHN	I say what's
MAN	Tell you
JOHN	What's the –
MAN	Feeling
JOHN	The story and
MAN	the gun.
JOHN	this.
MAN	weather.
JOHN	This is
MAN	anything
JOHN	This *is*.
MAN	tactics…
JOHN	What they
MAN	angle.
JOHN	Want to

MAN	Shot
JOHN	What they want to know.
	So.
	Sarah?
MAN	Sister.
JOHN	Oh.
MAN	Yeah.
JOHN	Not…
MAN	No.
JOHN	Oh.
MAN	Yeah.
JOHN	I'm
MAN	Okay.
JOHN	Sorry.
MAN	Yeah.
JOHN	But you
MAN	What?
JOHN	You see?
MAN	What?
JOHN	That's
MAN	Yeah.
JOHN	A story.
MAN	I get it.
JOHN	Guy who
MAN	I get it.
JOHN	Shot him.
MAN	Gets revenge.

JOHN	Revenge?
MAN	I get it.
JOHN	Is that –
MAN	What?
JOHN	What you…
MAN	No.
JOHN	Felt.
MAN	No.
JOHN	Revenge?
MAN	No.
JOHN	You said.
MAN	Your story not –
JOHN	Revenge.
MAN	Not mine.
JOHN	So when you –
	In the
	The
MAN	What?
JOHN	The moment.
MAN	No.
JOHN	When you.
MAN	No.
JOHN	Did it.
MAN	No.
JOHN	Did she?
MAN	No.
JOHN	You thought.

MAN	No.
JOHN	Of her?
MAN	Not at all.
JOHN	No?
MAN	A target. A mission. A target. A shot. No.
JOHN	Her face.
MAN	What?
JOHN	In those.
MAN	You don't –
JOHN	Those last
MAN	Don't care.
JOHN	Moments.
MAN	Do you?
JOHN	Pain.
MAN	Jesus.
JOHN	Death.
MAN	I follow.
JOHN	Do you.
MAN	Orders.
JOHN	Do you?
MAN	What?
JOHN	Feel?
MAN	What? Feel what?
JOHN	Do you feel?
MAN	I'm a guy.
JOHN	Guys feel.

MAN	I know.
JOHN	You do.
MAN	I do.
JOHN	You seem.
MAN	What?
JOHN	Cut off.
MAN	From.
JOHN	Feelings?
MAN	No.
JOHN	Emotions.
MAN	Next.
JOHN	Sarah.
MAN	Next question.
JOHN	Sarah.
MAN	Sarah.
JOHN	Your
MAN	Yeah.
JOHN	Sister, what would she.
MAN	Think?
JOHN	Yeah.
MAN	Of me.
JOHN	Yeah.
MAN	That I'm
JOHN	You're
MAN	The one.
JOHN	Yeah.
MAN	She'd be
JOHN	Yeah.

MAN	Glad.
JOHN	Yeah.
MAN	I'm alive.
JOHN	Okay.
MAN	she always
JOHN	What?
MAN	Said I'd
JOHN	Okay.
MAN	Die.
JOHN	Yeah.
MAN	In war, she said.
JOHN	Yeah.
MAN	War.
JOHN	Right.
MAN	But in the
JOHN	Yeah.
MAN	In the end it was her.
JOHN	Yeah.
MAN	In war.
JOHN	You think?
MAN	What?
JOHN	That that
MAN	What?
JOHN	– what happened
MAN	You mean
JOHN	Was that?
MAN	Yeah.
JOHN	War?

MAN	Looked like it yeah.
	Looked like war to me.
JOHN	You're married?
MAN	No.
JOHN	No.
MAN	You?
JOHN	What?
MAN	Tell me.
JOHN	What?
MAN	Why this?
JOHN	I don't.
MAN	Why me?
JOHN	You're
MAN	Why this?
JOHN	Important.
MAN	Two years.
JOHN	Yeah.
MAN	Two years.
JOHN	Two years yeah.
MAN	To find me.
JOHN	That's right.
MAN	Two years.
JOHN	Yeah.
MAN	Just this.
JOHN	That's right.
MAN	Why?
JOHN	The story.

MAN	Do you care?
JOHN	Do I care?
MAN	Or is it just –
JOHN	The story.
MAN	The man.
JOHN	Yeah.
MAN	Who shot.
JOHN	Yeah.
MAN	Bin Laden.
JOHN	Yeah.
MAN	Some story.
JOHN	Some story.
MAN	You'll be rich.
JOHN	No.
MAN	Famous.
JOHN	Yes.
MAN	Rich.
JOHN	Maybe.
MAN	No maybe.
JOHN	Maybe.
MAN	You will.
JOHN	Okay.
MAN	I want to know.
JOHN	What?
MAN	My question.
JOHN	What?
MAN	To you.
JOHN	What?

MAN   Do you?

JOHN   What?

MAN   Care.

JOHN   Care?

MAN   Yes.

JOHN   About?

MAN   Me. The shot.

JOHN   Yes.

MAN   The man.

JOHN   Of course.

MAN   Bin Laden.

JOHN   Look –

MAN   Revenge.

JOHN   Well

MAN   Do you.

JOHN   Okay.

MAN   Care.

JOHN   Okay.

MAN   Or is this just.

JOHN   Of course.

MAN   Is this just the way you –

JOHN   I'm American.

MAN   Is this just the way you make your mark?

JOHN   I'm as American as you.

MAN   Not nervous.

JOHN   What?

MAN   You were –

JOHN	What?
MAN	Nervous.
JOHN	Well –
MAN	Not nervous any more.
JOHN	You're a
MAN	What?
JOHN	Seal.
MAN	Yeah.
JOHN	The best.
MAN	Yeah
JOHN	Degree
MAN	Degree
JOHN	MA
MAN	Yeah.
JOHN	Languages
MAN	Four.
JOHN	Bright.
MAN	The best.
JOHN	So you must
MAN	What?
JOHN	Think.
MAN	Think?
JOHN	Yeah.
MAN	Think…
JOHN	About why?
MAN	What?
JOHN	Why it happened.
MAN	What the

JOHN	Yeah
MAN	The Towers
JOHN	Yeah, the –
MAN	The Pentagon.
JOHN	Yeah.
MAN	Do I know –
JOHN	What do you –
MAN	Why it happened?
JOHN	What do you –
MAN	Is that your –
JOHN	No.
MAN	Your question?
JOHN	Your thoughts.
MAN	My…
JOHN	Yeah.
MAN	My thoughts.
JOHN	Yeah…
MAN	Why?
JOHN	The readers.
MAN	The story.
JOHN	Unique. Viewpoint.

MAN	The things.
JOHN	Okay.
MAN	The things I believe.
JOHN	Yeah.
MAN	Are important.
JOHN	Okay.

MAN	For me.
JOHN	Yeah
MAN	My family.
JOHN	Yeah
MAN	My sister.
JOHN	Okay

MAN   Freedom to think, freedom to act, the rule of law, intellectual development, equality of opportunity, eradication of corruption, a free market, freedom to worship freedom to express your opinion if it does not inhibit other opinions, equality of men, of women, regardless of gender, race, or sexuality, the separation of church and state, the ability of every citizen to vote in free and fair elections to decide their own government, these things don't come free, these things have to be earned with war and blood, it's the only price. They said my sister was killed by the blast as the plane hit the building, they think she died quickly and I don't know I won't ever know for sure about that, but what I do know is that the man who ordered my sister's death did not want anything I could give him. I know that he was, according to the criteria I've just laid out for you, the enemy. He was the enemy of everything I believe. He was the enemy of everything that allows you to do your job and everything that keeps you safe and gives you life. He ordered the attack as retaliation, yes, but not against bombs or bullets but against music, and movies and sports and life. And my sister loves those things. I didn't kill him because he killed my sister, I didn't kill him because of the country he came from or what he believed, I killed him because I know what the enemy looks like and it had his face.

JOHN	Okay.
MAN	Okay.
JOHN	Thanks.
MAN	Yeah.

JOHN   Yeah.

MAN   You want –

JOHN   No.

MAN   Anything else?

JOHN   No.

MAN   Worth it?

JOHN   Yeah.

MAN   Two years?

JOHN   Yeah.

MAN   You're gonna be rich.

JOHN   Yeah.

MAN   With this.

JOHN   Yeah.

MAN   God bless.

JOHN   Yeah.

MAN   God bless America yeah?

JOHN   Yeah.

MAN   God bless America.

JOHN   God bless America.

MAN   Okay.

He goes.

VOICES FROM THE MOSQUE

Alecky Blythe

Characters

IMAM

TEENAGE MUSLIM

IBRASALIM

Note on the Text

This text has been created from conversations recorded with people interviewed at various London mosques. The edited interviews are played through earphones to the actors during rehearsals and performance. The actors do not learn the lines, instead on stage they listen to the edited interviews and copy exactly what they hear with precise detail, reproducing every cough, stutter and hesitation.

Day of Judgement

IMAM.

In Islam killing anyone is absolutely forbidden (*Beat*.) killing, *hurting* anyone – is absolutely forbidden. Killing is not, is not, is not *our* job. Allah Sumantala is the creator, he is, in the – in the day of judgement he will ask. 'I created my slave, who are *you* to kill?' and he has to answer 'Why did you kill him?' an every single (*Beat*.) dead people will come with their head on the hand and they will say to Allah 'Oh Allah ask him why did he kill me? Why did he kill me in this – in the world?' But they have to answer it, 'Why do people kill?' So it's very, very, very strong ya know. I just don't know why Muslim do that.

Nobody can hide in that day. And this is the day will be judged that this person will go Jana – paradise – or this person will go hell because of his deeds ya know an there – Whatever the Qu'ran Ayah says 'Al yawma nukhtimu aala afwahihim watakulimuna aydihim watashahadu arjuluhum bima' – that that day Allah Sumantala will ll-lock his mouth, his mouth cannot speak, his hand will e-speak, his feet will speak, his – ears will speak. A hand will say 'Allah he has done wrong thing with me, he has find someone, he has hurt someone.' The feet will say 'Allah he has taken him to the wrong places.' So everything – everybody – part of the body will speak. The person who has done wrong actions in this world – they will know automatically that I will be – punished.

To be honest I don't know wheth Bin Laden will be because – I don't know – if he's good or bad. I have never met him, I don't know who it is and where he's from. Ya know – what – How do you know hi – Bin Laden have killed 'em? (*Beat*.) Through media isn't it? This is what it is. (*Beat*.) This is what it is – we can't accuse someone unless we know the other person. Yeah videos. How do you know it's true? (*Beat*.) How do you know it's true. Serio – seriously. You could do anything with computer. (*Beat*.) Maybe Mr Bush can say 'I didn't do it.' But the day of judgement he wouldn't be able to hide anything because the hands gonna speak – his – everything is gonna speak – everything will come up. After the day of – end of this world, and the Muslim believes that end – there *is* an end of this world. Allah Sumantala will destroy everything and then the day of judgement will start. The skies will finish and it *is* coming to a end. That all these things are happening – *killing* and all this thing will start. This is what it is.

Bus Stop

IMAM.

Beause obviously I see when I go to airport, or to when I go to the er – train station bus stop, I see people are looking at me. Yeah – I think that – but I think it's just – they don't *know* me. They don't under*stand* me. Ya know. If they want to know me they should to talk to me they could ask me. 'What you-who are you – why do you *dress* like this?' Ya know, 'Wha – what do you *want*?' they should ask me. Then-they-they'll see – that I'm no different to – them. It's the same thing. It's jus that I believe in Islam and they don't. Ya know. But what they-the-the view that they are looking at me because they think that I victim or I'm – I'm – I'm like ya know terrorist or – but that view is *wrong* because they don – they haven't spoken with me. This is what it is. They should find out about Islam and Muslims before they-ya know – accuse – someone.

What I do is jus – wh-when I see – smiling is good. When I smile otherwise jus stay an – ya know – normal. You have to know people isn't it? Some people if you smile at them they might get more angry so you jus don't smile at them isn't it. You don't wanna make them more angry ya know. (*Beat.*) This is what it is.

Discrimination

TEENAGE MUSLIM.

We weren't seen like that before s'like there was no discrimination ya know, way before (*Beat.*) two thousand and one ya know. Since then it's like when you hear Islam – or a non-Muslim would hear Islam will think terrorist straight away and a terrorist is a person that comes to invade your land, takes over, ya know, rapes your women, kills your people. That's what a terrorist is basically that terrorises your whole – area right? – And Muslims are not terrorists. We're not terrorists ya know. They're going to kill the brothers and sisters in Iraq an that yeah basically they're defending their home. The word Islam means peace and it's a peaceful religion – it's very beautiful. (*Beat.*)

I go on the-on the train, people are watching me. They're – especially if I'm wearing that long dress. I've 'ad to tell people 'what the *fuck* you lookin at?' literally because it in*timi*dated me. I *am* a human bein – (*Beat.*) ya know. Peo – I've been intimidated by people where they've been looking at me like – 'Terrorist' ya know, people holding onto their bags ya know. I-I don't like these things. I might be on the train – It doesn't mean every person wearing that long dress that goes on the train is a bomber. Ya know what I'm tryin a say? I'm against these things. I – Ya know I actually love my life more than anything. I love my life, I'm not going to jeopardise my life for anybody else. Unless it's do with my mum, my sister, my family *only*. Nobody else – no one is worth it ya know. But – a lot of discrimination has been happening (*Beat.*) in England (*Beat.*) towards Muslims – definitely – a hundred per cent.

Curious

IBRASALIM.

Cos what happened after 9/11 is err – err – er amount of Muslim in the world is increased look in America now fifty thousand a *year* and is ten million Muslim and in Britain is nearly two million Muslim. Ya know why? The 9/11 ha-gave people to research more about Islam. (*Beat.*) You got it? You got my point? People are thinking who are the people who are bombing our building? So let me search about the religion. Is it really their religion? It made – it made people like erm – curious. People want to know, so they give them a purpose, they give them – they give opportunity for others. You understand? (*Beat.*) You got my point?

Twenty years, back twenty years ago there wasn't Muslim like that, (*Beat.*) there wasn't mosque like that. What is the success of Islam? Why? London is like – I don't know there is a lot of Muslim, it is the second religion in London. There's a lot of Muslim, there's a lot of places of worship. In Finsbury Park itself there is three mosque, in Highbury there is twelve – place of worship. In London maybe seven hundred and fifty – it's a lot. (*Beat*.) *Yes!*

I said the 9/11 benefited in one side the Muslim er community in Britain, (*Beat*.) in one side. For me it benefited me a lot. Because why, people a lot are coming to ask me about Islam in my work place, in court, in all the places I work, as public services people come to me they say 'Ibrasalim, what do you think about Bin Laden, like he's dead – do you think he's okay? Are you happy, are you not happy?' So-so people are er interested.

ELECTRIC THINGS

Adam Brace

Characters

OUDRY, *Congolese, forties*

PATIENCE, *his daughter, twelve*

BEATRICE, *her mother*

MAN

ANOTHER MAN

MEREDITH, *American, twenties*

RADIO

Setting

A hut in a village in North Kivu, East DRC.

Note on the Text

☐ *Empty silence – a silence in which there's nothing to say.*

■ *Full silence – a silence in which things are actively not said.*

1.

OUDRY *and his daughter,* PATIENCE.

PATIENCE *is in her bed.* OUDRY *sits with her.*

PATIENCE. One more and I won't say another word.

OUDRY. Not falling for that.

PATIENCE. I mean it, one more, you're so good at it.

OUDRY. And your mother's waiting for me to come to bed.

PATIENCE. She's not she's drinking next door with Mama Salima.

☐

OUDRY. You notice too much.

PATIENCE. Please.

OUDRY. Goodnight.

PATIENCE. *Please*.

OUDRY. Your brothers are back tomorrow and you must sleep so
  you can help feed them.

  He leans in to kiss her, she ignores him.

  What sort of ungrateful child are you?

PATIENCE. Please one a short one

OUDRY. You've heard them all before. Just remember one and tell
  it to yourself

PATIENCE. Why don't I tell you one. So I can practise, for my own
  children.

OUDRY. What do you mean practise.

PATIENCE. I mean, no I

OUDRY. What do you mean practise.

PATIENCE. I mean so I can get as good as you.

OUDRY *looks sternly at her.*

No, I didn't mean – no there's nothing.

OUDRY. Because if you have a child now you know where it's going.

PATIENCE *turns away from him and buries her head.*

Unless its father is a Prince. Or a Trader.

Then you know where it's going.

Maybe you've met a Trader?

If you've met a Trader, don't keep it yourself.

■ OUDRY *gets up, thinks about going and then sits back down.*

You'll have babies one day, when you are paired and things are easier.

■

Alright tell me a story tell me a *short* one.

PATIENCE *bounces back up.*

PATIENCE. Ha great which one is short?

OUDRY. I am too soft, seriously.

PATIENCE. How about Why the Crocodile Wouldn't Eat the Hen?

OUDRY. No no, far too long.

PATIENCE. The Television Singer Who Went to Europe.

OUDRY. That's *much* too long. And it's not a good story for a child.

PATIENCE. Well I'm not a child so that's fine

OUDRY. No.

PATIENCE. The Wasp Who Ate His Own Face?

□

OUDRY. I never told you this story.

PATIENCE. No I made it up.

OUDRY. Strange crazy child.

PATIENCE. The Kind Brothers Who Came Back from the Mine with a Necklace for Patience.

OUDRY. Alright now

PATIENCE. And beer.

OUDRY. Alright now I'm going to bed.

PATIENCE. No no a short one.

The Man who Sent the Birds from the Trees. Please?

And after I'll fall straight asleep.

Probably before the end even.

OUDRY. That is quite short. Go on then.

PATIENCE. Okay. The Man Who Sent the Birds from – (*Yawns.*)

She pretends to fall suddenly deeply asleep.

OUDRY *gets up to walk out, but* PATIENCE *springs to life
again.*

– the Trees.

In the beginning there was one man who planted all the trees.

And the man lived in a shimbec in the shade of the biggest tree in
the tallest forest, where you cannot even see the sky. And on the
trees there came much fruit. And the man ate the fruit, and his
family ate the fruit. And birds lived in the trees and also ate the
fruit.

OUDRY. Good start.

PATIENCE. Many years later, on the trees came less fruit. But the
men were used to eating whenever they wanted. They made drink
from the fruit and cooked the fruit and used it to throw at people
they didn't like

OUDRY. That's not in the story

PATIENCE. But they probably did

OUDRY. Get on

PATIENCE. And they wasted much fruit, because if you didn't eat it
quick it tasted like shit

OUDRY. No if you didn't eat it quickly it tasted *horrible*.

PATIENCE. Oh does shit taste nice?

He slaps her.

OUDRY. You call me a shit-eater!

PATIENCE. No. No sorry it was a question.

OUDRY. Tell this story like it matters, my grandfather brought this story from BaKongo.

PATIENCE. I'm sorry.

OUDRY. Hurry up then

PATIENCE. It tasted horrible. And now there was not enough fruit for both the men and the birds. So the son of the son of the son of the Tree Planter went to the birds and said 'No more fruit'. He told the birds that he owned the trees. And all the fruit. And if they lived in the trees then he owned them as well.

And many birds left and many birds starved but some birds continued eating the fruit. So the man left traps for the birds and killed some and even fed the birds to his family. And the birds hated the man. And one day, when the man was out walking, on a long walk, the birds flew down – Papa, how far do Cedric and Ben walk in one day?

OUDRY. They walk as far as they can get in daylight.

PATIENCE. Where do the rocks go?

OUDRY. Any reason to stay awake isn't it.

PATIENCE. Do they go to Bukavu?

OUDRY. Yes you can ask them about this

PATIENCE. How far normally?

OUDRY. It changes. It's about how many rocks the miners find, and how many the Commander takes. Ask your brothers about it tomorrow. When you've *slept*.

PATIENCE. Don't you know about it?

OUDRY. I know about it.

PATIENCE. There's tin something special inside the rocks Cedric says. And the Brigade will come to take them maybe

OUDRY. The rocks go the same way. The Brigade had the mine two years ago, then the Army took it back and maybe the Brigade will come again, but the rocks still go the same way.

PATIENCE. Where?

OUDRY. They say to Rwanda

PATIENCE. And then after that?

OUDRY. It's sold. Things are made with it.

PATIENCE. And does it heal people who have been shot?

OUDRY. No no, you can't find healing rock round here.

PATIENCE. And will they use it to build a tunnel from here to Europe?

OUDRY. No no, this rock is going to America to rebuild the two towers.

PATIENCE. Two towers?

OUDRY. They are two enormous towers in a city that were smashed one day by crazy pilots.

PATIENCE. I never heard of that

OUDRY. I saw television of it in Bukavu. Amazing, the tall towers falling to the ground on fire it was very beautiful actually.

PATIENCE. And that's where the rock goes, to build two towers smashed by crazy pilots?

OUDRY. Yes I dunno that's what people say am I in America?

PATIENCE. I'd love to meet an American.

OUDRY. Huh.

PATIENCE. Maybe tomorrow you can tell me the story of the two towers?

OUDRY. It's not a story, there is no story two planes hit two towers. They fell down. I don't know anything else.

PATIENCE. When?

OUDRY. Lord, maybe two years ago – *finish*!

PATIENCE. While the man was on a long walk all the birds flew back to the trees. Because they saw he was now old and weak and had no son and could not make them leave. And so the man ate less fruit. And that is why the birds are still in the trees.

OUDRY. Good you know it quite well.

PATIENCE. Thank you

OUDRY. And you do listen. Although the story doesn't really make any sense.

There are yells in the distance.

OUDRY is suddenly alert.

■

They listen.

■

There are more yells. They listen again. They look at each other.

OUDRY springs up and grabs food.

He pulls PATIENCE out of bed by her arm, it hurts her. He grabs a T-shirt and wraps food into it and presses it into her stomach.

Run for the bush. Don't come back for two days.

More yells and voices outside.

The door of the hut opens.

They look up at the door. BEATRICE runs in.

PATIENCE. Mama.

OUDRY. Is it, is it?

BEATRICE. It's the brigade, they are raiding. Patience run now!

PATIENCE looks at her mother then her father and runs out of the door.

OUDRY. And you too.

There are more yells, growing nearer.

BEATRICE is scrabbling for food, OUDRY helping her.

BEATRICE is just turning to run out of the door as a man forces his way in.

He is a MILITIA MAN, tall and raggedly dressed, a Kalashnikov slung casually over his shoulder. He stands looking at them.

OUDRY and BEATRICE start throwing all their food and possessions in front of him.

BEATRICE. There you go there you go, take it all.

He stands still. He looks at them.

■ *There are now loud screams and gunshots in the near distance.*

Another MAN *enters holding* PATIENCE.

BEATRICE. She is diseased, she is diseased!

The MAN *laughs.*

And points his rifle at OUDRY.

MAN. You are first.

2.

PATIENCE *is sitting tightly cross-legged on the floor of the same hut.*

MEREDITH *is sitting next to her with a notepad. She is an American in the uniform of the International Medical Corps.* MEREDITH *speaks imperfect French with* PATIENCE *and English with the radio.*

■

■

MEREDITH. If I look quick, I can help.

■ PATIENCE *shakes her head.*

■

Your mother, she say I look,

no uh, she say I *can* look.

■

She did.

■ MEREDITH *goes to* PATIENCE *and looks at her hair.*

May I touch?

PATIENCE *thinks and nods.* MEREDITH *strokes her hair.*

PATIENCE *slightly takes her hands from in front of her knees.*

MEREDITH *very delicately parts* PATIENCE*'s legs and inspects her wounds. It is very quick.*

Thank you very much. We can help you.

MEREDITH *hands* PATIENCE *some water, takes out a radio and stands up to leave.*

I go, two minutes. I am only outside. No one is leaving you alone.

PATIENCE *shakes her head. She looks imploringly at* MEREDITH.

■

You understand English?

PATIENCE *shakes her head slightly.*

MEREDITH *sits down. And takes out a radio.*

Okay so can you understand what I'm saying *now*? If I'm speaking English do you understand me? Anything?

PATIENCE *cannot understand.*

Okay, fine.

I stay.

PATIENCE *is glad to hear this.* MEREDITH *reads into radio in a deliberately calm and clear voice.*

Receiving? Over.

Girl thirteen fourteen mother maybe late thirties. Two brothers work at the tin mine, meant to return today, haven't yet. Husband beaten broken nose and eye swollen shut. Wife raped by two men. Daughter by six including probable forced rape by Father. Probable EB2. Suspected insertion of bayonet. Fistula. Severe bleeding stemmed by improvised rag. Recommend PEP kit. Over.

RADIO. Can Mother walk, over?

MEREDITH. Just about, over.

RADIO. Send to clinic, treat only emergencies on ground over.

MEREDITH. Received over.

RADIO. Daughter emergency over?

MEREDITH. Daughter emergency yes over.

MEREDITH *puts the radio down and sits with* PATIENCE.

■

PATIENCE. You were talking then about the rocks?

MEREDITH. Again?

PATIENCE. You are here for the rocks?

MEREDITH. Uh no, I don't understand, 'Ro–?

PATIENCE. The rocks from the mine.

MEREDITH. Rocks? Oh no I don't want rocks from the mine, I'm
here to help *you*.

PATIENCE. Are they to build your two towers the rocks?

MEREDITH. To build my towers? No the rocks don't build towers.

PATIENCE. Oh.

MEREDITH. The rocks build other things. Electric things.

PATIENCE *nods blankly.*

□ MEREDITH *leans in to help her.*

SPEED DATE

Ben Ellis

Characters

TERRI, *female, forty-two*

DATES, *male, variety of ages, varying around Terri's age, five of them*

Note on the Text

Kuala Lumpur, Malaysia

We catch each date after the introductions.

Date 1

TERRI. okay so how would you describe yourself? that's a terrible
question you'll have to forgive me i get so nervous at these things
i scratch myself i scratch myself a lot it's the eczema you see i
was in dubai for a few years and that made the whole thing a
whole lot worse like there's no difference between me and the
sandstorms just two clouds ha! so there you go i ask you a
question and i talk about myself i'd like to think that i'm proud
and elegant but what field do you work in

DATE 1. procurement

Short silence.

TERRI. do you smoke?

DATE 1. i'm an ex-smoker

TERRI. you don't really like me, do you?

DATE 1. i've only just met you.

TERRI. but you do know, straight away, don't you, like walking into
the house you're going to buy. fate.

DATE1. i don't believe in fate

TERRI. what do you believe in?

DATE 1. i like going to movies.

TERRI. you have interesting eyes

DATE 1. thank you.

Silence.

TERRI. we must have time for you to compliment me

The bell sounds to indicate change of partner.

Date 2

DATE 2. so what are you reading at the moment?

TERRI. I don't really have the time to read

DATE 2. what do you do?

TERRI. numbers. you know, numbers in the right places

DATE 2. right. financial. why not go to singapore?

TERRI. singapore's too much like london. even the powerpoints.

DATE 2. the plugs? they're the same here in malaysia too

TERRI. I mean, i need to be somewhere different before i settle down. and kuala lumpur's a very exciting city

DATE 2. like with the towers?

TERRI. never thought about them.

DATE 2. the architecture's based on the pillars of islam, do you know that? that explains some of their beauty

TERRI. you have very interesting eyes

DATE 2. we don't get much time to know each other, do we?

TERRI. then let's cut to the chase: how do you feel about children?

DATE 2. i'm too cynical to have children. won't be a good father. try not to be.

TERRI. cynicism is the only way to bring a child into this world. the only safe capsule. get torn to shreds otherwise. if moses was born today he would've been wrapped in cynicism not a blanket. cynicism or irony.

TERRI *has begun scratching herself furiously. She looks to be in some discomfort. A bit of skin flaking off.*

DATE 2. are you okay?

TERRI. yeah, yeah, no, it's, i'm just, i'm just very itchy, sometimes i could tear my skin off, how would that look? You come on a speed date and here i come, skinning and scalping myself right at you. Some sort of sight that would be

DATE 2. do you take drugs for it?

TERRI. they make it worse in the long-term.

DATE 2. have you tried not using soap?

TERRI. everybody asks that.

DATE 2. we're running out of time

TERRI. darling i'm forty-two i know i know i know

The bell sounds.

Date 3

TERRI *and the* DATE *have been silent for some time. And it's getting very awkward.*

TERRI. what do you think of the wine?

DATE 3. it's alright.

TERRI. bit minerally

DATE 3. is that a word?

TERRI. look it up

DATE 3. I'm more of a lager drinker

TERRI. then what are you doing with the wine?

DATE 3. you have to try different things, don't you

TERRI. but at what point, at what point do you stop doing that, say, this is where I've got to in life, and this is my decision, that's the one and i'm staying with that

DATE 3. but it's life. things keep changing. tastes keep changing. can't hold on to the one thing for ever

TERRI. then what are you doing here?

DATE 3. the woman in front of me changes every five minutes. brilliant

TERRI. you're a bit weird, aren't you

DATE 3. my friend keeps saying that

TERRI. your friend

DATE 3. yeah, I've only got one. he's over there

TERRI. does he keep changing?

DATE 3. only when we go out. he's very clean like that

TERRI. this isn't going to work

DATE 3. depends. you'll probably like my friend

> TERRI *scratches her arm, and the* DATE *notices the 'debris' and gets alarmed.*

> euw

TERRI. it's eczema

DATE 3. have you tried not using soap?

TERRI. oh i bet you say that to all the ladies

Date 4

TERRI. all i want sometimes is just one big man, a tall man, to hold me and cradle me, as if I'm a child again, some child in his world, and i mean sometimes, i mean, you seem tall, you looked tall when you stood up to come over here. Height can be wonderful. I mean, it can all go wrong, can't it, different ideas about love or sex or medicine – do you smoke? I smoke – and i had one guy i was pretty serious about who left me because of naturopathic medicines – i can't keep putting steroids on my skin because that will just weaken it, it won't flake but it'll bleed and cut and if you put a light bulb behind me i would glow like a lampshade that's what those creams do in the end, but he didn't want to understand, he said, 'why bother with natural medicines if you're going to smoke so much?' but how could he know? How could he know what it's like to be me? He can't he just can't

DATE 4. people don't empathise

TERRI. exactly

DATE 4. i had a girlfriend who left me because she said i didn't empathise

TERRI. my god what did you do?

DATE 4. tried to see it from her perspective

TERRI. ha ha

DATE 4. seriously and i've changed a lot since then. I reinvented myself. You're right. i accepted my height, and i seemed to grow taller. I empathised with people and they began to understand me.

TERRI. deep. Tall and deep. What would you want from me?

DATE 4. the dream. A garden. Swing set in a back yard. Being able to hear bird song in an evening glow, arm around my family

TERRI. that gigantic arm

DATE 4. yes

TERRI. and?

DATE 4. nothing else.

TERRI. nothing

DATE 4. you're disappointed

TERRI. no. no… it's…

DATE 4. what's not perfect?

TERRI. nobody no nobody moves in that picture… where are the fireworks? The big moments? What stands out?

Date 5

TERRI *has now had her glass of wine refilled several times and has lost count.*

TERRI. life

DATE 5. yeah

TERRI. it's just one thing after another

DATE 5. isn't it?

TERRI. should be. so

DATE 5. yes

TERRI. what's your plan for me, mister?

DATE 5. my plan?

TERRI. your thing. blow me away.

DATE 5. i wouldn't call it a plan. i'd call it talking. i had planned to talk.

TERRI. talk talk. we can talk forever, we can go nowhere forever. what are you putting on the table right now?

DATE 5. you're upfront

TERRI. it's taken me a while. don't ask about my eczema, it's a disaster and it's ruining my outfit. don't tell me to avoid soap, you wouldn't believe the shit i've tried washing my excuse for skin with. i'm drunk, i'm fed up, you look vaguely handsome, a little bit kind, a touch of steel so what are your plans for me?

DATE 5. plans? plans... for you?

TERRI. what's the blueprint, you know. where do you see me in ten years' time fuckface?

DATE 5. you're very aggressive.

TERRI. nah nah assertive yes know that i want you to want. there used to be a something here. there used to be something that i thought was ME here and that's disappeared and gone and i want to have a child i mean i don't want to die not having had a child and soon there'll be years and years of waiting do you understand what i mean by that? i suppose not although you'd better watch out better your sperm degrades as you age too – i want something else strong and alive and seething and noticeable in this place in this place in this place that was me a new me but one that doesn't overwhelm me

DATE 5. so it's children you're talking about?

TERRI. it's not just... it's not just... life should be just one thing after another that's what it should be, like a series of rides at a theme park, or a series of photos or like art work in a gallery, just...

DATE 5. one thing after another thing

TERRI's *flaking is now becoming surreal and unstoppable as she speaks the following:*

TERRI. yes and each thing should just reach out and grab and get your attention. without anything ever bad happening after. spectacular things. no particular order. it's such a good thing i must have been blessed to be the one who did the coffee run bang bang a plane goes into your building and what are you going to do but have this image this image of an image being destroyed and i don't want to talk about that because because if you try to make meaning from it you become me but it was spectacular and spectacles have to be in your life and they have to be spectacular. i'm ruins. look.

She lights up a cigarette.

it's like dandruff of the soul look at it. sorry i don't normally talk about it

DATE 5. that's pretty messy, Terri

TERRI. but it's making you look. hey it's making everybody look

DATE 5. you can't smoke in here

TERRI. i'm adding to the effect. watch it fall. watch it all come down and off you. are you going to love me again? is there ever any chance you could love me again?

DATE 5. tonight's the first night we've met

TERRI. you know me. look at my face. i'm every woman you ever wanted to build on and you've fallen out of love with me. you can love me again. i want you to know you can love me again. build the rest of your life on me.

DATE 5. let's get a doctor for that

TERRI. you can't put the thing you lost back in, simon – it has to be new and special. it has to be. it has to be strong. tall. like i was, si. we were something weren't we. so it has to be special. it had better be nothing if it's not not not special

TERRI *is now a vision of a collapse, a kind of after-the-collapse, smoking, fuming, all manner of debris around her, from her, but her eyes remain very clear.*

GIFT

Ella Hickson

Characters

JASON

WOMAN

KAREN

WOMAN 2

Jason is dark-skinned.

Jason is from Panama but passes as Arab.

Jason is in his mid-twenties.

Jason grew up in the southern states of America.

Jason wears a WTC TOUR cap and T-shirt.

One

JASON *stands at the gift counter. A pale* WOMAN *approaches.*

JASON. Hi. How can I help?

WOMAN. The tours – are – uh –

JASON. Quarter past, half past and quarter to; if you stand by the meeting point just in front of the blue door a guide will come to collect you at the appropriate time.

WOMAN. Do I buy tickets from you?

JASON. No. I can do you gold and silver lapel pins, patches, caps, coins, tribute pens, postcards, ornaments for your tree – in season; we got books, beer mugs, magnets, T-shirts and right now we have a special on these pins right here –

WOMAN. Thanks but I'm good.

JASON. Okay.

WOMAN. Just a ticket for the walking tour.

JASON. The cashier, by the blue door.

WOMAN. Thank you.

JASON. No, no – thank you.

The WOMAN *exits.*

JASON *stands.*

Beforehand they look – right through me. You see her, look right through me? Perfect and made-up, arranged a little… like… a doll – and they appreciate the chivalry, with the coats, the manners they like… sure, but beforehand they, they – look right through me.

Two

JASON (*voice-over, with real ring-a-ding*). 'Ladies and gentlemen, today's tour will be taken by Karen. Karen is one of our longest running guides here at The Tribute Centre, she has been working the Ground Zero tour here for a little over six years, yes six years, so you will be very well looked after indeed; couldn't be in better hands. Please gather by the blue door where Karen is waiting for you. She will be able to answer all of your questions. We do hope you enjoy the tour and have a good day.'

Three

JASON. The woman with the pale face joins the back of the group. She's alone… minus her coat she looks a little… skinned; like she might burn, somehow. She seems kinda in a rush, this is on her list and she'd like to get it ticked – that's what Karen says, Karen says you can spot a list-ticker… but I'm not so sure – she seems a little – a little…

It was her husband, Karen's – I mean. Karen still cries, every tour, every time. Six years; same spot. She points up at the space in the sky where the window that he jumped from should be. She gives a few statistics, smiles at them… silence… then tears. They have to have personal stories of the event, the tour guides, so I wasn't allowed – I was gift shop only because on the day, at the time of the – I was playing RuneScape and then later jerking off which I guess people wouldn't pay ten dollars to hear about.

Sometimes on my break I follow the tour a while. Today I hang back a little so as Karen can't see me. My girl – the pale-faced – is part of the silence. She doesn't seem in a hurry any more. I think – yeah, she – I think I can see her… crying, a little.

Four

JASON. Hi.

WOMAN. Hi.

JASON. How was –

WOMAN. Yeah.

JASON. Would you like a –

WOMAN. How much are the pins?

JASON. Plain silver – ten dollars, plain gold are twelve – the flags are –

WOMAN. That's kind of expensive.

JASON. The 'Never Forget' ones are less; limited edition – end of line.

WOMAN. Right.

JASON. Are you – ?

WOMAN. Oh yeah – I'm fine.

JASON. Would you like a tissue? Your face is still damp.

Beat.

WOMAN. Thank you.

> JASON *hands the* WOMAN *a tissue. He threads his fingers through hers a little and holds on a little longer than he should. The* WOMAN *takes a sharp little breath inward.*

Beat.

> It's the bit at the window – that – the idea of looking down and – deciding to – deciding that doing something is better than just... waiting.

JASON. You think of the lovers right?

WOMAN. What?

JASON. All the people you've slept next to. I always think, in that situation, I'd measure my life by the heartbeats of the people that I'd slept alongside.

> *The* WOMAN *seems suddenly cold.*

Would you like your coat? I can get your coat for you, if you'd like – or a baseball cap – you know you lose ninety per cent of your heat from...

The WOMAN *smiles.*

WOMAN. You know any place nearby that does tea or hot chocolate or – ?

JASON. Sure. (*Beat.*) I mean – I'm nearly done here – so I – can – show you if –

Five

JASON. There's this woman that stands, oftentimes, at the back in Karen's tours. I've seen her once or twice but the guys have said she's in like once a month, only ever for Karen. And when Karen is at the window point – talking about how her husband jumped, and she starts to cry – this other woman gets this look – this look of like, pure angry and then she starts crying too and the two of them just stand there and stare at each other with wet faces. I watch from the gift-shop window, and sometimes I think that one day, when the tour has stopped and the grass has grown and there are hover-boards or some shit, Karen and that woman – will still be standing, just staring at other, pure angry and crying – neither one of them wanting to be the first to stop. I feel like they'll just be there, face to face, for the rest of time.

Six

A bar – they have not had tea. There are drinks on the table.

JASON. Karen says I sell so much because I'm the only thing in the whole shop with a heartbeat and that's what people want when they come out – they want something with a heartbeat that's able to smile at them.

WOMAN. Put you in their pocket.

JASON. That's what Karen says.

WOMAN *puts her hand onto his chest.*

WOMAN. You make me look whiter.

JASON. Yeah, I guess I do.

WOMAN. What do you sell most of?

JASON. Erasers.

WOMAN. That's funny.

JASON. Is it?

JASON *slides his hand up her thigh.*

WOMAN. Where are you from – your family, originally?

JASON. I – uh –

WOMAN. Are you a – ?

JASON *kisses the woman.*

Seven

JASON. I think about it sometimes, like – why. And I figure it's like
if you went round Auschwitz – I suppose – you know – if you
were a Jew you might be inclined to fuck a German just to – just
so – so you didn't just stand there staring at each other pure
angry and crying for the rest of time, you know?

Eight

JASON. Hey Karen.

KAREN. Hey Jase – how you doing today, honey?

JASON. Good thanks.

KAREN. How's your mum doing? She still here?

JASON. No, she's gone back home.

KAREN. Panama, right?

JASON. Yeah, Panama.

KAREN. You know I didn't even know where Panama was, couldn't
'a told ya – it was just the hats in my head.

JASON. Yeah – people do that.

KAREN. Your ma showed me – right at our back door, and I had no
idea. I always thought you were from – from – ya know – over –
in a – over – ya ma, I liked her, she was nice, I liked her.

JASON. Yeah, she's good.

KAREN. How's things selling?

JASON. Good. The stationery is still going real well.

KAREN. Yeah? Them limited-edition pins?

JASON. Still got a whole heap.

KAREN. Look at that smile.

JASON. Tch – stop it Karen.

KAREN. You found yourself a nice young lady yet, Jase? You need
a nice young lady – you know? It matters.

JASON. Yeah?

KAREN. Matters more than anything else.

JASON. You think so?

KAREN. Like I always say – end of the day – you measure your life
by the heartbeats of the people that you've slept alongside. Huh?
(*Kisses* JASON *robustly on the cheek and ruffles his hair.*) You
find yourself a nice young lady – okay?

JASON. Okay Karen.

KAREN. Get home safe.

JASON. Okay Karen.

Nine

WOMAN 2 *approaches*.

WOMAN 2. Hi can I get a postcard?

JASON. Sure – we got the double icon right here, the towers and liberty – or we got the flag, or the panoramic sunset – in blue or red – or the 'far but not forgotten' which is the liberty again but kinda... miss?

WOMAN 2. Um – I – I'm not – uh –

JASON. Sure. Are you –

WOMAN 2. Sorry?

JASON. Would you like a tissue?

WOMAN 2. Well – yeah – thanks.

JASON. You just done Karen's tour?

WOMAN 2. Yeah – it's um – it's real – real – um –

JASON. The bit by the window –

WOMAN 2. Yeah. I just don't know how you – what you – uh – to be able to – the things you'd think – I –

JASON. I think you'd think of the lovers.

WOMAN 2. What?

JASON. All the people you've slept next to. I always think, in that situation, I'd measure my life by the heartbeats of the people that I'd slept alongside.

WOMAN 2. You think?

JASON. Yeah.

> JASON *hands her the tissue and holds her hand a little long. He wipes a tear from her face and she takes a sharp little breath inward.*

Ten

JASON. I'd say two-in-ten success rate or thereabouts. I think there have been now, working here five years, about seventy, in all. I know the ones to try with; their faces are still a little damp. Like dolls, plastic – like someone held 'em over a flame, they've melted a little.

Beat.

You have to get used to them crying during – it's kind of – I don't know, they just do that.

Beat.

I sometimes think what they'd look like all together – all laid out on their backs – like – if it would fill a football field... like, they'd look like – like swimmers – their legs all bent back – gasping – dolls – melted a little – then set all crooked; their bones too... unforgiving.

Beat.

I don't hear from them again ever.

Like not one. I sometimes think that's weird.

They know where I work, right?

Beat.

Recently I try to slip one of the 'never forget' pins in their pockets, before they go.

I think it's nice.

They're not selling that well anyways.

Beat.

And I always put their coat back on for them – real gentle –

And they appreciate the chivalry.

They're real grateful... for the kindness.

They are.

OLIVE GARDEN

Samuel D. Hunter

76

Characters

MAN 1

MAN 2

MAN 3

MAN 4

MAN 5

WOMAN 1

WOMAN 2

WOMAN 3

WOMAN 4

WOMEN 5

WOMAN 6

WAITER

*The immediately recognisable interior of an Olive Garden
restaurant, specific enough that we know exactly where we are but
general enough that it could be any Olive Garden around the
country (excluding those in New York, Washington, Los Angeles, or
any other major, well-chronicled urban area). Throughout the scene
there is the steady sound of bad, fake Italian music playing in the
background.*

*In the back above the bar is a large flat-screen television that you'd
expect to normally play football. The characters may look at it
casually throughout the scene, but none of them focus on it for any
extended period of time. To them it's simply a part of the architecture
of the space.*

There are five tables of varying sizes on stage. At Table 1 are: MAN
1 *and* WOMAN 1. *At Table 2 are:* MAN 2 *and* WOMAN 2. *Table
three:* MAN 3, WOMAN 3, WOMAN 4. *Table four:* MAN 4,
WOMAN 5, WOMAN 6. *Table five:* MAN 5, *alone, on his cell
phone. There is one* WAITER, *this is his entire section.*

*There is already food at Table 1, Table 3, and Table 5. Table 4 has
yet to order, Table 2 is ordering as the scene begins.*

*The effect should be that none of the conversations ever cease, the
actors continually talk throughout the scene. The scripted dialogue
is just the words that come out over the din of the larger
conversation, the bits and pieces that the audience is piecing
together from the chaos.*

*The scene starts suddenly, like we're being thrown into the middle of
something that's already been going on for a while. The television
plays a commercial for Mop 'n' Glo or something.*

WAITER *is at Table 2.*

WAITER. – the 'Tour of Italy', which is lasagna and / fettuccine –

MAN 2. There's meat in that?

WAITER. The lasagna? Yes.

MAN 2. Good.

WOMAN 4. DAD.

MAN 3. WHAT?!

MAN 4. How is that racist?! I'm not being racist.

WOMAN 6. You're being racist.

MAN 4. You don't even know any black people. Besides he's mostly white.

MAN 5. I'm just sort of sick of the whole thing if you really wanna know what / I think –

MAN 3. – something about a 'total transmission flush', and I told him –

WOMAN 3. Well maybe you needed it.

MAN 3. But it – that's not even a thing, a 'total transmission flush'? That's not a thing.

WOMAN 3. Well.

WOMAN 4. DAD.

MAN 3. WHAT?!

The television switches from commercials to an annual 9/11 memorial ceremony, the reading of the names at Ground Zero. It's not evident which anniversary it is, just that it's the anniversary. This continues in the background throughout the scene.

WAITER. Alright. And I'll keep the salad coming.

WOMAN 2. Thanks so much!

The WAITER *goes to Table 4.*

MAN 5. – but they just don't want us to know, it's all this big fucking thing they don't want us to know about –

WAITER. We actually do have gluten-free pasta.

MAN 4. It's cardboard. Tastes like cardboard.

WOMAN 6 (*mortified*). YOU BE QUIET.

WOMAN 4. THEY HAD CRAYONS LAST TIME.

MAN 3. I DON'T KNOW.

WOMAN 2. So are you a Virgo? I'm really good at these things, I can always tell.

MAN 2. Nope.

WOMAN 2. Are you sure?

MAN 5. – I mean explosives on the side of the thing, and – YEAH THAT'S WHAT I'M SAYING –

MAN 1. Don't make them sing. I don't want you to make them sing. Didn't like last year.

WOMAN 1. Oh Dad. Grumpy grump!

MAN 1. Don't make them sing.

MAN 3. So you think I should just give them all my money, is that what you're saying?

MAN 4. She doesn't drink.

WOMAN 6. I just wanted a taste! He offered a sample!

WAITER. It's a white zinfandel. It's bright and flavorful. A full bottle is only $14.95, or you can buy one of our Famiglia Sized Carafes for only $24.95.

WOMAN 2. Capricorn?

MAN 2. No.

WOMAN 4. DAD WHAT'S THE SOUND A WALRUS MAKES IS IT LIKE *NUUHHHNNNNN* –

MAN 3. ADULTS ARE TALKING.

MAN 5. – because so much of this stuff just doesn't make any goddam sense, they had, you know, *experts* or whatever saying that it doesn't make sense –

MAN 1 *is opening a wrapped present.*

WOMAN 1. It's a Chia. It's shaped like a head.

MAN 1. I don't understand.

WOMAN 1. Now you have something to take care of!

MAN 1 *pulls out a pack of cigarettes.*

WOMAN 3. – Katie's cousin or something, she was working in New York at the time I guess, she said –

WOMAN 1 (*re: cigarettes, to* MAN 1). *Put those away.*

WAITER. Should I just come back – ?

WOMAN 6. No, you don't / need –

MAN 4. Yeah, why don't you give us a few more minutes.

WAITER. Take all the time you need!

WAITER begins to exit, dropping the carafe of wine. It crashes onto the ground.

(*Louder than he intends.*) *Shit!*

Everyone stops, looking at him. For the first time everyone has stopped talking, and the names from the television can be heard, underscored by the terrible Italian music playing in the background.

TELEVISION (*slow and deliberate*). Loretta Ann Vero. Christopher James Vialonga. Matthew Gilbert Vianna. Robert –

WAITER (*to everyone, meek*). I'm sorry. I'm just so sorry.

Embarassed, the WAITER quickly picks up the pieces of the plate and exits. The din resumes.

WOMAN 4. WHAT DID HE JUST SAY?

MAN 3. NO ONE HEARD HIM.

WOMAN 2. Aries?

MAN 2. Please stop.

MAN 1. There are genocides going on right now, you know.

WOMAN 1. I know something else we can talk about!

MAN 1. People being *killed*. Women being *raped*.

WOMAN 1. Ellie is pregnant again! Did I tell you that?

MAN 1. Yes.

WOMAN 1. Well she is!

MAN 3. Oh my gosh that's so awful.

WOMAN 3. I know.

MAN 3 (*sotto voce*). Maybe we shouldn't be talking about it / around –

WOMAN 4. WHAT ARE YOU GUYS TALKING ABOUT?

MAN 3. NOTHING.

*The volume of the whole restaurant seems to crescendo,
everyone's speech seeming to grow just a little quicker, a littler
more high-pitched.*

MAN 5. – going all the way up to the top, all these / questions that –
What, you don't think our government is capable of that?!

MAN 4. He told me himself! He told me he was a Muslim!

WOMAN 6. WELL YOU MISHEARD HIM.

MAN 1. I fucking hate it here.

WOMAN 1. DAD DON'T USE THAT WORD.

WOMAN 4 *climbs on top of the table.*

MAN 3. GET DOWN RIGHT NOW.

WOMAN 2. I just don't know how you could even vote for
someone like that!

MAN 2. Because I have a brain, that's why.

WOMAN 4 *playfully jumps off the table, falling onto the
ground.*

MAN 3 (*to* WOMAN 4). YOU'RE AN EMBARRASSMENT. I
MEAN YOU'RE EMBARRASSING US.

MAN 5. Maybe if you just opened your eyes a little! Maybe if you
would've finished high school like I did you wouldn't be such a
fucking retard!

WOMAN 5. Mom stop! Sometimes I just want to run away!

WOMAN 6. YES WELL MAYBE YOU SHOULD.

MAN 4. ALRIGHT EVERYONE ENOUGH. IT'S A DAY OF –
TODAY IS –

MAN 2. Well maybe that works for some people, people living in a
magical fairyland –

WOMAN 2. Oh so I'm living in a magical fairyland because I think
that –

*The lights go off in the restaurant. Suddenly, all conversation
ceases, everyone is suddenly still.*

TELEVISION. Celeste Torres Victoria. Joanna Vidal. John T.
Vigiano II. Joseph Vincent Vigiano. Frank J. Vig –

The WAITER *enters with a piece of cake with a lit candle on top. He starts to sing, everyone more or less joins in half-heartedly.*

WAITER, *et al* (*singing*).
Happy birthday to you,
Happy birthday to you – (*Etc.*)

MAN 1. What did I say? What did I just tell you?

WOMAN 1. Oh grumpy grump!

MAN 1. I fought in Korea. Stop singing.

The singing finishes, the WAITER *puts the cake in front of* MAN 1. *The conversations resume.*

WAITER. Happy birthday! Today you're part of our *famiglia*!

WOMAN 1. Blow it out!

WOMAN 4. MRS. BAKER-WILKINSON SAYS I'M GOING TO –

WOMAN 3. Honey nobody likes a loud person.

MAN 5. OPEN YOUR EYES YOU RETARD.

MAN 4. WOULD IT BE RACIST IF I SAID A WHITE PERSON WAS 'UPPITY'?

WOMAN 6. STOP.

WOMAN 5. Dad stop being racist! I don't feel good!

MAN 1. – didn't have clean drinking water, wearing the same underwear for months –

WOMAN 1. Okay I have no idea what you're talking about. Just blow out the candle.

MAN 1. Maybe I don't want to blow out the fucking candle.

WOMAN 4 *gets back up on the table.*

WOMAN 3. Honey –

MAN 3. GET DOWN.

WOMAN 4. DOES THAT MEAN SOMEONE IS GOING TO KILL ME SOMEDAY?

WOMAN 3. No, honey, it just means… It just means that –

WOMAN 1. DAD JUST BLOW OUT THE GODDAM CANDLE ALREADY.

WOMAN 4 *jumps off the table, toppling down onto the floor.*
MAN 1 *finally blows out the candle. Everyone claps.*

WAITER. *Abbondanza!* We won't charge you for the cake! If the rest of you would like to join in it's only $2.95 a slice!

MAN 5. I'M HANGING UP NOW. BYE-BYE, FUCKFACE.

MAN 5 *angrily hangs up his phone, leaves some cash on the table, and exits.*

WOMAN 2. Well obviously Alice was mistaken about us.

MAN 2. Yeah I guess she was.

The WAITER *goes to Table 5, collecting the money.* MAN 3 *grabs* WOMAN 4, *forces her to sit at the table.*

WOMAN 4. BUT WHY?

WOMAN 3. Honey I just told you that nobody likes a loud person. Let's change the subject.

MAN 1. Take me home.

WOMAN 1. God, Dad, you're eighty-five years old and this is how you're going to act?

MAN 1. Just take me home.

MAN 3. Yes, let's change the subject. I'm sick of talking about it.

The WAITER *enters, bringing food to Table 4. He eventually goes to Table 5, clearing it off.*

WOMAN 1. Alright, you want to be a miserable old man, fine. Sorry for trying to make your birthday happy.

WOMAN 1 *signals the* WAITER *for the check.*

WOMAN 2. So you're fine with everything that's going on? It's all just – *fine* with you?

MAN 2. It's saving American lives. So, yes.

WOMAN 4. NO BUT I JUST –

WOMAN 3. Quietly.

WOMAN 4. No but I just –

MAN 3. I thought we were changing the subject?

WOMAN 3. I'm trying.

MAN 4. I'm sorry.

WOMAN 6. Okay.

MAN 4. Honey I said I'm sorry. I SAID I'M SORRY.

WOMAN 6. AND I SAID OKAY.

MAN 4. GOD you know what?! I'm done. See you at home.

MAN 4 storms out. The WAITER *brings the check to Table 1.* WOMAN 1 *pulls money out of her purse and leaves it with the check.*

WOMAN 2. I just can't even talk to you. It's like I don't even know what you are. I can't even see you.

WOMAN 5. I think I need to go to the bathroom.

WOMAN 6. Are you making yourself throw up again?

WOMAN 5. MOM.

WOMAN 6. If you're making yourself throw up –

WOMAN 5. MOM PLEASE.

The WAITER *takes the check for Table 1.* MAN 1 *and* WOMAN 1 *get up and start to leave.*

WOMAN 1. Every year it's like this. I'm just trying to make this day happy! That's all!

MAN 1. Just take me home.

The WAITER *brings the check to Table 2.*

WAITER. Thanks guys! Have a great day!

WAITER *starts to clear off Table 1.*

MAN 2. I got it.

WOMAN 2. Oh no you don't.

MAN 2. Whatever.

WOMAN 5. Mom I really feel sick.

WOMAN 6. I'm not letting you go to the bathroom if you're just going to make yourself throw up.

WOMAN 6 *signals* WAITER *for the check.* WAITER *nods and exits with the dishes from Table 1.*

MAN 1. I'll drive.

WOMAN 1. No you won't.

MAN 1. I can still drive.

WOMAN 1. No you can't.

>MAN 1 *and* WOMAN 1 *exit together.*

WOMAN 4. Did I make everyone sad?

WOMAN 3. No honey.

MAN 3. Jesus can we please talk about something else?

WOMAN 3. What do you think I've been trying to do?!

>WOMAN 5 *vomits on the table.*

WOMAN 6. OH MY GOD WHAT IS WRONG WITH YOU?!

>MAN 2 *and* WOMAN 2 *get up to leave.*

MAN 2. Do you want a ride?

WOMAN 2. Fuck you.

MAN 2. Okay.

WOMAN 2. *God I just hate everything about everything.*

>WOMAN 2 *and* MAN 2 *exit, separately. The* WAITER
>*re-enters with the check for Table 4. He sees the vomit, stops
>momentarily.*

WAITER. Oh.

WOMAN 6. We just had. It's a little accident.

WAITER. Oh, sure! Just, uh…

>WAITER *leaves the check on Table 4, exits quickly.*

>WOMAN 6 *quickly pulls out her purse and puts some bills down
>on the table.*

WOMAN 6 (*sotto voce*). *Why did you just do that?! What's wrong
with you?!*

WOMAN 5. I'm sorry.

WOMAN 4. I'm sorry.

MAN 3. What are you sorry for?

WOMAN 4. I'm just sorry Dad. Sorry.

WAITER re-enters and cleans up the vomit.

WOMAN 6 (*to* WAITER). Thank you.

WOMAN 6 hurriedly collects her things and pulls WOMAN 5 out of the restaurant.

Silence apart from the reading of the names on the television and the Italian music. The WAITER clears Table 4 and exits. The television continues under the Italian music.

TELEVISION. Matthew Blake Wallens. John Allice, Jr. Barbara P. Walsh. James Henry Walsh. Jeffrey P. Walz.

MAN 3. Nothing's going to happen to you, okay? Or me. Or your mom.

TELEVISION. Michael Warchola. Stephen Gordon Ward. James Arthur Waring. Brian G. Warner.

WOMAN 3. Who was that over at that table? Was it what's-his-name, Don and Ashley's kid?

MAN 3. I don't know.

WOMAN 3. I think it might have been.

WOMAN 4 is silent, staring down.

TELEVISION. James Thomas Waters, Jr. Patrick J. Waters. Kenneth Thomas Watson. Michael Henry Waye.

The WAITER re-enters.

WAITER. Hey there! How was everything?

MAN 3. It was fine. Thanks.

WAITER. Can I interest you in any dessert? Cheesecake, ice cream, molten chocolate / lava –

MAN 3. I think we're fine.

WAITER. Okay great then. I'll just leave this with you, but you folks feel free to take your time!

MAN 3. Uh-huh.

The WAITER leaves the check, exits. MAN 3 takes out his checkbook, writes a check. WOMAN 4 continues to stare down.

TELEVISION. Dinah Webster. Joanne Flora Weil. Michael T. Weinberg. Scott Jeffrey Weingard.

WOMAN 3. How much are you leaving?

MAN 3. It's fifteen per cent.

WOMAN 3. Is that / enough – ?

MAN 3. It's fifteen per cent.

MAN 3 finishes writing the check, puts it on the table. He pauses for a quick moment.

Okay?

MAN 3 and WOMAN 3 get up.

WOMAN 3 (*to* WOMAN 4). C'mon.

WOMAN 4. . . . I'm sorry. . .

MAN 3. Oh just stop it.

MAN 3 and WOMAN 3 exit with WOMAN 4 in tow.

The WAITER re-enters and clears Tables 2 and 3 as the television and the Italian music play in the background.

TELEVISION. Vincent Michael Wells. Timothy Matthew Welty. Christian Hans Rudolf Wemmers. Ssu-Hui Wen. Oleh D. Wengerchuck. Peter M. West. Whitfield West, Jr. Meredith Lynn Whalen. Eugene Whelan. Adam S. White. Edward James White III.

Finally, the space has been completely cleared of people, food, plates, and utensils. The WAITER stands in silence looking at the empty space.

James Patrick White. John Sylvester White. Kenneth –

The WAITER takes a remote control out of his apron and turns off the television.

GROUNDED

John Logan

Characters

MOTHER

DAUGHTER

PRODUCER MAN

PRODUCER WOMAN

GIRLFRIEND

BOYFRIEND

MOM WITH KIDS

FLIGHT ATTENDANT

MIDDLE EASTERN MAN

TEXAN

'JOHN'

'PAUL'

OTHER PEOPLE IN TERMINAL

Setting

September 11, 2001.

Crowded airport terminal.

Note on the Text

At 9:37 a.m. on September 11 American Flight 77 hit the Pentagon.

Eight minutes later the FAA ordered all commercial flights grounded, and shut US airspace for the first time in history. All flights were cancelled and every aircraft in flight was ordered down.

Approximately 4,500 flights were grounded and more than 350,000 passengers were stranded in airports across the nation.

At 11:00 a.m. on September 13 the FAA allowed some airports to reopen.

With grateful thanks to The Day the World Came to Town: 9/11 in Gander, Newfoundland *by Jim DeFede, which gave me the idea.*

J. L.

Darkness.

We hear airport PUBLIC ADDRESS*:*

PA VOICE.… United 17 to Wichita cancelled… Delta 2112 to Orlando cancelled… American 48 to Chicago cancelled… Continental 1285 to Kansas City cancelled… Southwest 446 to Los Angeles cancelled…

Lights up.

People everywhere. Contorted around uncomfortable airport chairs. Sleeping in corners. Wandering. Drinking. Crying. Huddling.

Trying to make sense.

MOTHER *stands ramrod straight, gazing up at an unseen TV. Her* DAUGHTER *is right there with her.* MOTHER *never moves, just stares up at the unseen TV.*

Waiting.

Vague news reports from 9/11 come from the TV like distant white noise.

DAUGHTER. Come away… Come away.

MOTHER *won't go. Just stares up at the TV.*

PRODUCER MAN *is talking to his associate:*

PRODUCER MAN.… If it's not Bruce Willis we're fucked you understand that? There's no way we're gonna get the CGI budget without a star. This is just the reality of the world now: it's a whole new world. Everything gotta be CGI.

PRODUCER WOMAN. We're on it. His people are on it. We're all over it. You need to relax.

PRODUCER MAN. You keep saying that…

PRODUCER WOMAN. He's not the only star out there.

PRODUCER MAN. He's the one we got on the hook. Stars don't get on the hook. They spend their whole lives getting *off the hook.*

PRODUCER WOMAN.... What about Keanu?

PRODUCER MAN. Keanu can only open a *Matrix*, zero box-office beyond.

GIRLFRIEND *has been crying*.

She turns to her BOYFRIEND:

GIRLFRIEND.... I just don't understand this.

BOYFRIEND. The world's fucking cruel, what's to understand?

MOM WITH KIDS *is holding her two sleeping children*.

MOM WITH KIDS. Excuse me, language.

GIRLFRIEND. Sorry. Sorry.

A uniformed FLIGHT ATTENDANT (*male or female*) *is patiently explaining to someone, for the hundredth time:*

FLIGHT ATTENDANT. I just work for Southwest, I don't have any information. Sorry.

GIRLFRIEND. I don't think the world's cruel. That's not fair.

BOYFRIEND. Then how do you explain this?

GIRLFRIEND. I can't.

BOYFRIEND. God. Doesn't. Care. It's random. Life's random. You need more evidence?

DAUGHTER (*to* MOTHER). We called Sarah, there's nothing we can do. Come away. It doesn't do you any good to see this...

MOM WITH KIDS (*glances to TV*). God, why do they keep showing that?!

DAUGHTER.... Please, just sit down. Sarah will call.

MOTHER *won't go*.

Meanwhile, A MIDDLE EASTERN MAN *is speaking in Arabic into his cellphone. He's concerned.*

A TEXAN — *jeans, boots, Western accent* — *watches him closely... Finally approaches and stands near him 'casually'.*

'JOHN' and 'PAUL' enter. They carry guitar cases and are dressed as The Beatles, circa 1964. Grey uniform, Beatle boots, Beatle haircuts. Authentic Liverpool accents.

JOHN. No better here.

PAUL. No better elsewhere.

JOHN. Make do with here?

PAUL. Better than there.

Some people notice them. They are a bit self-conscious. Find a place to sit/lounge.

PRODUCER MAN.... I've been trying to get his agent. Phones are all messed up. Or that's the excuse they're going to use anyway.

PRODUCER WOMAN. You should call him directly.

PRODUCER MAN. Oh just call him directly. That's good. You don't call Bruce Willis directly.

PRODUCER WOMAN. I meant the agent.

PRODUCER MAN. Point is: we're stuck in butt-fuck when it's all going down in LA. They're going to be at the Four Seasons in ten minutes having the fucking oatmeal with dried currants and deciding my fate, the entire fate of the rest of my life.

PRODUCER WOMAN. That's kind of dramatic.

PRODUCER MAN. You don't know.

PRODUCER WOMAN (*re: 9/11*). Maybe they'll cancel the meeting.

PRODUCER MAN. That's New York. What does LA give a shit?

MOM WITH KIDS. Excuse me. Excuse me. Language. Kids?

PRODUCER MAN *looks at her like she's a Martian.*

BOYFRIEND (*re: PAUL and JOHN*). Just when this day couldn't get weirder.

GIRLFRIEND. Wanna go talk to them?

BOYFRIEND. No.

GIRLFRIEND. I'm going to.

BOYFRIEND. Don't.

GIRLFRIEND. Why?

BOYFRIEND. It's stupid.

FLIGHT ATTENDANT *goes to* DAUGHTER *and* MOTHER *at the TV.*

FLIGHT ATTENDANT. Anything new?

DAUGHTER. No.

They stare at the TV for a moment.

How long do you think we'll be grounded?

FLIGHT ATTENDANT. I just work for Southwest. I don't really have any information. Sorry.

DAUGHTER. Of course, yeah.

FLIGHT ATTENDANT. This has never happened before. No one knows.

DAUGHTER. Is anything taking off?

FLIGHT ATTENDANT. No… I keep thinking of my friends in the tower.

DAUGHTER *looks, surprised.*

Oh no. I mean the control tower… Air-traffic control. All their screens must be blank. There are no blips, no planes. Just… green.

DAUGHTER. I wish someone would tell us something.

FLIGHT ATTENDANT. I'm sure they're doing everything they can… Where were you headed?

DAUGHTER. Tampa for a wedding… (*Explains.*) That's my mom. Her son… my brother… works in the north tower.

FLIGHT ATTENDANT. Jesus.

DAUGHTER. He had the flu. Was off work a few days… We're not sure he went in today. We called his wife but… I mean, nothing.

FLIGHT ATTENDANT. What can I do? You want a drink?

DAUGHTER. Yes I want a drink.

FLIGHT ATTENDANT *goes.*

Meanwhile, the MIDDLE EASTERN MAN *has finished his call, watches the TV. The* TEXAN *leans in.*

TEXAN. Can I ask you a question?… Is it true about the virgins?

MIDDLE EASTERN MAN *stares at him*.

You give your life for Allah and you go to heaven and there are all these virgins waiting; hundreds of virgins just waiting on you. Is that true?

MIDDLE EASTERN MAN. What?

TEXAN. I'm South Texas Pentecostal myself — and we have us some unusual practices I will admit, including the handling of serpents — but we sure as hell got nothing like those virgins.

MIDDLE EASTERN MAN. Excuse me.

He walks away. The TEXAN *isn't satisfied. He keeps an eye on the* MIDDLE EASTERN MAN.

Meanwhile, GIRLFRIEND *goes to* JOHN *and* PAUL.

GILRFRIEND. I give up. What?

PAUL. Tribute act.

GIRLFRIEND. Just the two of you?

PAUL. George and Ringo are on another plane.

JOHN. On the way to Reno. Which sounds like a song.

PAUL. Casino gig.

JOHN. Which doesn't.

GIRLFRIEND. Are you really English?

PAUL. Even better. Real Liverpudlians.

GIRLFRIEND. Oh. I love The Beatles.

PAUL. Thank you.

JOHN. Thank you?

PAUL. You know what I mean.

PRODUCER MAN (*on cellphone*). . . . uh-huh, uh-huh, uh-huh... I wonder if you're seeing the bigger picture here, Doug. This is a franchise opportunity. He needs a franchise since the *Die Hard* movies are kaput – no, no, you're right, he doesn't *need* anything, sorry sorry... (*Listens, gestures to* PRODUCER WOMAN*: 'This guy's killing me.'*) Well, will you get back to me?... Okay, okay, right... (*Glances at TV.*) Yeah. It's awful.

Fuck Saddam, right?... Who?... No we're stuck at the airport...
uh-huh... You'll call me as soon as you talk to Bruce, right?
Cool.

He hangs up.

He was on the treadmill. My whole life is going down the drain
and he's on the fucking treadmill. Doesn't even have the decency
to stop jogging.

FLIGHT ATTENDANT *returns to* DAUGHTER *with two drinks.*

FLIGHT ATTENDANT. I got an apple juice and I got a vodka.

DAUGHTER *takes the vodka and drains it.*

DAUGHTER. My brother works on the 87th floor. Unbelievable
view of the... Did you see them falling? Or jumping?... His
name is Scott.

She starts to cry. FLIGHT ATTENDANT *comforts her; moves
her away from* MOTHER *so as not to upset her.*

GIRLFRIEND. Do you always dress like that?

JOHN. Like what?

PAUL. Came right from a gig to make the red-eye, which we missed
anyway. Normally we don't dress like this.

JOHN. Normally we dress like Sergeant Pepper.

GIRLFRIEND. Are you on a tour?

JOHN. Seedy motels and casinos. We're not the best Beatles out
there.

GIRLFRIEND. Are there a lot?

JOHN. Locusts.

PAUL. We saw an act in Atlantic City you would swear was them.

JOHN. Even the George.

PAUL. George is the hardest.

JOHN. But it's our chance to see your country. When you're from
England, you grow up watching America on the telly. I swear we
came over and thought everything was going to be like *Dynasty.*

PAUL. With those lovely Joan Collins shoulder pads.

JOHN. But it's not.

PAUL. Which you probably know.

JOHN. *It's better*. You know what's great about America? No one gives a shit. You walk through Times Square dressed like the f-ing Beatles and everyone's like — shrug — 'good for you, man'. That ought to be your national motto: Good for you, man.

DAUGHTER's cellphone rings. She jumps.

Steps away, answers, talks privately.

FLIGHT ATTENDANT *stays close.*

PRODUCER WOMAN. Bruce is getting a little long in the tooth for action parts.

PRODUCER MAN. Bruce Willis is five years younger than I am.

PRODUCER WOMAN. I wouldn't cast you either.

PRODUCER MAN. You're hysterical.

GIRLFRIEND. You've had the best of our country then.

PAUL. 'Good for you, man.'

JOHN. Last month we were playing at the Holiday Inn in Albuquerque.

PAUL. A name to die for.

JOHN. And all the power went out. Some wind storm in the desert.

PAUL. The desert! You have deserts!

JOHN. All the lights go out, but there's candles on the tables, so there's a wee glow. Just enough to make out the faces. We were going to stop, but they wouldn't leave, they kept calling for more. So we kept on playing. Went through our whole set, with everyone singing along in the dark.

DAUGHTER *hangs up.*

She prepares herself, carefully goes to MOTHER *and speaks quietly.*

DAUGHTER. Mom… I talked to Sarah… She doesn't know anything yet, so don't, um… Scotty went into work today. His cold was feeling better and, um, he went into work. This doesn't mean…

She trails to silence.

MOTHER *looks at her. Takes in the news… Her resolve's shaken, but not broken… She turns back to the TV.*

GIRLFRIEND. Why don't you sing something?

JOHN. Not right. This day's not right for singing… Keening maybe.

MOM WITH KIDS *turns to them.*

MOM WITH KIDS. How long do you think we'll be here?

GIRLFRIEND. I don't think anyone knows.

MOM WITH KIDS (*re: her sleeping kids*). I don't know what to tell them about what happened. What do I tell them? I don't have the words.

JOHN. Maybe there are no words.

MOM WITH KIDS. I have to make them up then… (*Looks at the TV.*) I tried to keep them from seeing too much, but, you know, they were just showing everything live… This is what they're going to think the world is. *This.*

She's upset.

There's a lot I don't understand these days. But this I really don't understand. So how am I going to explain it to them?

GIRLFRIEND *comforts her.*

BOYFRIEND *approaches.*

BOYFRIEND. You want something to eat?

GIRLFRIEND. Not right now. Jesus.

BOYFRIEND. I'll bring you something.

GIRLFRIEND. I'm not hungry.

BOYFRIEND. I'll bring you something.

He goes.

MOM WITH KIDS. Thank you… I'm sorry.

GIRLFRIEND. Don't be sorry.

MOM WITH KIDS. My husband hates it when I get emotional. Sorry.

She turns back to her children.

GIRLFRIEND. 'Hates it when I get emotional…'

JOHN. You could weep.

Beat.

GIRLFRIEND *looks around, takes it all in*.

GIRLFRIEND. I feel like we're in limbo. No one telling us anything. Stuck here. Who knows how long.

PAUL. With fluorescent lights.

JOHN. If you're Catholic, limbo literally means 'the edge of hell'.

GIRLFRIEND. Do you think that's what this is?

PAUL. It's the edge of something.

GIRLFRIEND. But what?… And if we're at the edge of something we can step back, right? It's like in tarot cards, the 'death' card doesn't really mean death; it means change. Maybe it's even good change. Maybe that's what this is: the death card.

JOHN. So do you go forward or not? How do you know?

GIRLFRIEND. I think you just know… Something happens and you know… On the TV, when I see all that dust swirling around like snow and the smoke over New York I imagine all those new souls going up and watching us. Maybe they'll tell us.

JOHN. Maybe.

PAUL. Do you believe in angels?

JOHN. Why live if you don't?

PAUL. Generally, I believe in hobbits. And Quaaludes.

The TEXAN *goes again to the* MIDDLE EASTERN MAN.

TEXAN. Don't get me wrong, I think it's great. Mostly the Christian idea of heaven sounds pretty boring. Shit, no virgins waiting up above in the Good Book, you follow?

MIDDLE EASTERN MAN. Do you have something to say to me?

TEXAN. Hey, Aladdin, take it easy.

MIDDLE EASTERN MAN. What did you just—?

TEXAN (*re: 9/11*). Big day for you guys.

MIDDLE EASTERN MAN. What the fuck is that supposed to mean?!

TEXAN. They're saying it's Iraq.

PRODUCER MAN (*on cellphone, a bit desperate now*).... I'm not sure you understand the significance of what's going on here, Doug. This is big. This is game-changing. People are going to remember this for ever and tell their kids about it and... uh-huh, un-huh... *Because it's a fucking science-fiction franchise.*

PRODUCER WOMAN. Shhh.

TEXAN. They're saying it's terrorists. Islamic extremists. I'm not making this shit up!

The MIDDLE EASTERN MAN *walks away again. Trying to avoid the confrontation.*

PRODUCER MAN (*on cellphone*). What?! Of course it is... Two movies *is* a franchise!

He moves away restlessly, continues more quietly.

GIRLFRIEND. First time I remember hearing The Beatles was at my mom's house in Michigan. My folks are divorced and I was staying with her for the Christmas break and she had all these old records. Like actual wax. She put on *Abbey Road* and sang all the songs. She was feeling really depressed and it cheered her up. It was snowing outside.

JOHN. You know we're not really The Beatles.

PAUL. They're a fair piece older.

JOHN. And I'm actually dead.

GIRLFRIEND. But you're here today for a reason. The towers, you, me, all of this... It's not just random... It can't be.

PAUL. She's one of those spiritual girls, John.

JOHN. You know what they do to me, Paul.

GIRLFRIEND (*smiles*). I mean it... Something like this – today – it makes you stop for a second, doesn't it? Today — everyone stops... No more planes flying... No more stupid gossip at the water cooler... No more mean jokes... Everything matters... I matter and you matter and I'm here for a reason and you're here for a reason.

JOHN. What's the reason?

She looks and him, smiles.

GIRLFRIEND. You'll know.

The PRODUCER MAN *finally hangs up his cellphone and returns to* PRODUCER WOMAN.

Slumps next to her.

PRODUCER MAN. So it's a pass. He's doing some war movie… Studio's going cold on the whole project apparently.

PRODUCER WOMAN. So we go to Keanu. Or somebody else. We go to Denzel. This is a franchise, everyone wants a franchise.

PRODUCER MAN. There's this moment, this one moment when things stop and you either make critical mass or you don't. You could hear it in Doug's voice. This morning was the moment and nothing happened.

PRODUCER WOMAN. Hey, there's always tomorrow.

PRODUCER MAN. There is no tomorrow for this one.

Beat.

I turn fifty this year. I got two kids in school and a mortgage you would not believe… So what happens now?

FLIGHT ATTENDANT (*explaining patiently to someone*). I just work for Southwest. I don't have any information. Sorry.

JOHN. I'll remember this.

GIRLFRIEND. What?

JOHN. Here, this morning. I didn't bring a camera to America on purpose, so I would be forced to actually experience things, not spend the whole trip trying to line up shots of the White House, you know? It's funny what you remember: those faces in the dark in Albuquerque; the trash under a bridge in New Orleans; this man walking a dog along this long highway in Oklahoma; this girl in the airport.

Meanwhile, the TEXAN *moves to the* MIDDLE EASTERN MAN *again.*

TEXAN. Lemme tell you, buddy, when we find out who pulled this shit you can goddamn well be sure we are going to bomb you back to the frickin' Stone Ages. You better hope there are a lot of virgins up there. We are going to fuck you up.

A tense beat… The TEXAN *finally moves away.*

The MIDDLE EASTERN MAN *is deeply disturbed by the encounter. He pulls out his cellphone to make a call – but his hands are shaking so much he can't dial the number. Finally he stops trying.*

The BOYFRIEND *returns to* GIRLFRIEND, JOHN *and* PAUL.

He has candy.

BOYFRIEND. It's crazy over there. They're running out of food already. This bitch had like bought out the whole place, like the world was ending. She couldn't even carry it all. I got Twizzlers and some other crap.

He gives her some candy. She offers to JOHN *and* PAUL.

GIRLFRIEND. You want something?

JOHN. Wouldn't say no.

PAUL (*loves the word*). Twizzlers!

BOYFRIEND. They say there might be more at the next terminal. There's a MacDonald's. Let's go see.

GIRLFRIEND. No this is good.

BOYFRIEND. Come on. I'm hungry.

GIRLFRIEND. Our flight's here.

BOYFRIEND. It's just the next terminal. No one's taking off. I want real food. *Come on.*

JOHN. We'll save you a spot in limbo.

BOYFRIEND. Hey, that's okay. Don't worry about it, Ringo.

PAUL. Ouch.

GIRLFRIEND *stands.*

GIRLFRIEND. I need to go.

JOHN. Sure.

GIRLFRIEND. Later.

JOHN. Yeah… Hey, what's your name?

She smiles.

GIRLFRIEND. Eleanor.

She goes with the BOYFRIEND. *But they stop a bit away. She's having a serious conversation with him.*

Meanwhile, DAUGHTER*'s cellphone rings again. She jumps again. Answers.*

She moves away as she speaks privately.

MOM WITH KIDS *turns to* JOHN *and* PAUL.

MOM WITH KIDS *(re:* BOYFRIEND). That guy's a jerk.

JOHN. The heart wants what it wants.

PAUL. Very sage.

MOM WITH KIDS. My husband used to talk to me like that. Then one day he started complaining about dinner, not hot enough, not fast enough, same old same old. And something inside me just snapped. In my heart, I knew it was the moment I had to do something. I didn't say anything. I just quietly got the kids and got into the car and drove to the airport. That was yesterday.

PAUL. Good for you, man.

JOHN. Where are you going?

MOM WITH KIDS. Anywhere.

DAUGHTER *slowly hangs up her cellphone.* FLIGHT ATTENDANT *watches.*

DAUGHTER *holds it together. She goes to her* MOTHER *and whispers to her.*

Beat.

MOTHER *screams. She collapses to the floor. It's harrowing.*

DAUGHTER *and* FLIGHT ATTENDANT *comfort her.*

MOTHER *keens for her dead son.*

Everyone watches.

No one moves.

Pause.

Then…

JOHN *opens his guitar case.*

Removes his guitar.

He plays six notes. They resonate. They're familiar.

He plays The Beatles' song 'In My Life'.

PAUL *joins in.*

They quietly sing.

GIRLFRIEND *steps away from* BOYFRIEND.

She stands there alone and joins them singing.

MOM WITH KIDS *joins in.*

More and more.

The song ends.

It's brought some comfort.

The End.

THE SENTINELS

Matthew Lopez

Characters

ALICE

KELLY

CHRISTA

WAITRESS

Setting

The Sentinels takes place in a coffee shop a few blocks from Ground Zero in Lower Manhattan, save for the final scene which takes place at the Windows on the World restaurant at the top of the North Tower of the World Trade Center.

The play spans ten years, moving backward from the present. Each scene takes place on the anniversary of September 11, save for the final scene, which is set a year before the attacks.

1. September 11, 2011

A coffee shop, not at all fancy.

ALICE *and* KELLY. KELLY *is very pregnant.* ALICE *shows her pictures of a baby on her iPad.*

ALICE. Oh, and this is bath-time.

KELLY. How adorable!

ALICE. I think there's…

> ALICE *flips through. It seems like picture after picture are the same with only slight movement of face and hands between them. There are literally hundreds of the same thing. Almost like a movie in slow motion.*

> Well, it's all the same, really. I take a lot of pictures. You'll understand soon.

KELLY. We're already taking pictures of everything. The room as we've been preparing it, my belly as it's been growing.

ALICE. You take pictures of your stomach? No.

KELLY. Yes! To track the progress. It's… I don't know. How often do you get to do this?

ALICE. As often as you want.

> You look well.

KELLY. I am WONDERFUL.

ALICE. And your, um, husband –

KELLY. Jeremy.

ALICE. Jeremy. He's, ah, excited?

KELLY. Tickled pink. (*Makes a happy realisation.*) Which is actually the name of the shade we painted the room.

ALICE. You're having a girl.

KELLY. We're having a girl.

ALICE. It's so nice to see you thriving.

KELLY. That's the word! That is the word. Yes. Thriving. I, ah…it was hard to – well, impossible, really – to imagine ever being happy again. I couldn't…and yet… (*Points to her abdomen.*)

ALICE. Tickled pink.

KELLY *smiles, looks lovingly at her baby bump. Then a pause.*

KELLY. Oh, this old coffee shop! It's strange to be back here. Was it always this… (*Whispers.*) down at the heel? My goodness. I wasn't sure I'd come. It was Jeremy, actually, who convinced me.

ALICE. I'm glad you're here.

KELLY. I have missed these pancakes!

She digs in ferociously. The WAITRESS *enters with more coffee, sees her tearing into her pancakes, smiles, looks at* ALICE, *gives a knowing look, then exits.* KELLY *misses this entire exchange.*

I can't believe how fat some of the other wives have become.

ALICE. Kelly!

KELLY. Well, haven't they? Or maybe you don't notice it because you see them more often than I do. At meetings and – do you still, um, go to –

ALICE. I do, yes.

KELLY. Well.

ALICE. It's comforting. Still. After all these. And it's not just for support. Not just. We've accomplished / quite a lot in the last few years.

KELLY. I know you have. You have all been amazing. Watching over us all while we go about our lives. Always vigilant. You keep the flame burning.

ALICE. You're the only person I know who could use words like 'vigilant', and not make me feel I'm being mocked.

KELLY. I'm not / mocking you!

ALICE. I know, that's why I said –

KELLY. I'm mocking those fats who waddled down to the service today.

ALICE. Kelly!

KELLY. Being a widow is no reason to let yourself go.

ALICE. Well you…

KELLY. This is different and you know it! And besides, I'm not a widow any more.

ALICE. You'll always be a widow.

Silence.

KELLY. So Christa's not…

ALICE. No.

KELLY. Have you –

ALICE. Not for two years.

KELLY. Oh.

ALICE. Her choice.

KELLY. Yes. Well, again, you are ever vigilant. Even if some people want to forget. You will never let us.

Pause.

Show me some more pictures.

ALICE *picks up her iPad and begins flipping through more photos of her granddaughter.*

2. September 11, 2010

ALICE *sits by herself, eating blueberry pancakes. The* WAITRESS *stops by and refills her coffee. The* WAITRESS *gently touches* ALICE*'s shoulder as she exits.*

3. September 11, 2009

ALICE *sits by herself again. The* WAITRESS *passes and takes a look around, then sits down across from* ALICE. *He takes off her shoes and kneads her tired feet. She's almost lost in her own world. She then looks up and catches* ALICE *watching her. Embarrassed, she starts to put her shoes back on.*

ALICE. Don't worry. You're tired, I'm sure.

WAITRESS. If you only knew.

ALICE. I'm embarrassed to say that I don't know your name. After all these years.

WAITRESS. Don't sweat it. That ain't your job. I had a guy who came in every afternoon at 3:30 for a cup of coffee and a slice of pie. Monday through Friday, without fail, for years. Always paid cash, never stayed more than fifteen minutes. It got so that I didn't have to look any more. Something in my body clock knew it was time to pour some coffee and slice up some pie. Even on my sick days which – thank you very much – were and remain few and far between, there'd be an itch around 3:30. He'd usually order apple. Cherry, if we had it but only if it was fresh. So, you know, he didn't get cherry all that often. And he knew. Oh boy, did he know. He'd send it back – 'this tastes like Tuesday,' he'd say. That's what he'd say. 'This tastes like Tuesday.' In all those years, I never could get a Tuesday slice past Thursday afternoon. He just knew. For years. Then one Tuesday he stopped coming in. He was here that Monday and then… (*Slaps her hands together.*) gone! Just like that. And I never knew his name. 'Slice of Pie and Coffee Man,' I called him. You're my 'Once a Year Widow.' I hope you don't mind. We have names for customers.

ALICE. I don't [*mind*].

WAITRESS. Where's, um…well, we called them Blueberry Princess and Whiskey Dragon.

ALICE (*cannot help but laugh*). They couldn't make it this year.

WAITRESS. Well, I'm glad to see you again. Even though I'm sorry that you're here.

ALICE. Yes, I…

WAITRESS. I got tables need tending. I'll get you some more coffee on my way back round.

ALICE. Okay, um, thank you.

WAITRESS *starts to exit.*

I'm –

WAITRESS *stops.*

Alice. My name is Alice.

The WAITRESS *smiles and exits.*

4. September 11, 2008

ALICE *and* CHRISTA *together.* CHRISTA *shouts into her phone while clutching a whiskey. A bowl of untouched soup in front of her.*

CHRISTA. I'm sorry, Jessie, but you've had three weeks to do this assignment and you've said nothing to me about it and now suddenly it's an emergency. Well, it's your emergency, not mine. Figure something out.

Because you do this to me all the time and I'm sick of it.

ALL THE TIME, Jessie, and it's getting old.

I don't know what to tell you, Jessie, I can't do anything about it from here.

I don't wanna hear about it.

I don't wanna hear about it!

You made your bed, kiddo, you gotta lie in it.

It's an expression.

It's an expression.

Well maybe you should actually make your bed one day and then you'll know.

Look, I gotta go. My lunch is melting. We'll talk about this tonight.

She hangs up, lets out a groan, then takes a giant swig.

Jesus Christ, it never ends! Drama, drama, drama, that's all I get from morning till night with that kid. Sometimes I just wanna throw her out a goddamned window. I thought moving to a real house in a real neighborhood would calm her down. It just gave her more doors to slam. You and Charlie were lucky you had boys. Hell is a house filled with teenaged girls. That one, most especially. And when her sister gets there, ohmygod. I think I'm just going to let those two have the house and I'm going to move back to Brooklyn. I'll pay the neighbors to toss in raw meat and a Jonas Brothers CD and not open the door until they're old enough for college. That fucking Peter really knew what he was doing, leaving before they got so horrible. Not that he was ever helped out when he was alive, but still. How did you get those boys off to Harvard and – where was it? – Stanford? God love you – without help? Well, you had your sisters. That was a lucky break. And you had boys. That, I think, was your best decision.

She takes a big gulp, finishes, looks for the WAITRESS, *signals for another.*

God, what does it say about my life that this is what I look forward to for fun?

The WAITRESS *brings her another drink. She takes it without thanking her and takes another greedy gulp.*

What a turnout, huh? Who knew all we needed was a Presidential election to get the people to show up? Who you gonna vote for? I like that Palin. She's an idiot but, man, can she wear red.

Pause.

How you been, Alice? I can't believe we let a whole year go by.

ALICE. I tried.

CHRISTA. I know you did, baby. You're very good about that. I'm sorry, it's all my fault. These girls, they're all I've got time for. It's insanity.

Her phone rings again. She answers it.

I don't wanna hear it!

She hangs up, takes a gulp.

How are the boys?

ALICE. The boys are fine. Marcus just started law school.

CHRISTA. Already? (*Whistles*.) Time flies, huh? So you still rattling around in that big ol' house all by yourself?

ALICE. Yes, Christa, I am.

CHRISTA. You should move to the city! You're a single woman.

ALICE (*deeply offended*). I am NOT a single woman!

CHRISTA. No, I mean… you know what I mean. Live a little. God knows you can afford it.

ALICE. I am fine where I am. There might be grandchildren one day. They'll need a big house to run around in.

CHRISTA. Breaking all your things, scuffing up the floors. No. Thank. You.

Hey, how's Kelly? You ever hear from her?

ALICE. We speak on the phone once a week.

CHRISTA. You do? She never calls me. How is she?

ALICE. She seems happy. They bought a small house.

CHRISTA. All the way on the other side of the world. Good for her. God, I'd love to get the fuck outta here.

Pause.

Listen, I just want you to know that this is probably going to be my last year doing this.

ALICE. This?

CHRISTA. The memorial and all. At least for a while. I'll probably hit the big ones every now and again but I can't keep doing this every year.

ALICE. It's one day a year.

CHRISTA. I know, but still. Year in, year out, what's the point?

ALICE. The point –

CHRISTA. And for how long? I mean, I know the point. I know. I just don't see the point any more. You know? I don't need to… I just don't need to keep coming back. Dressing all in black, going back down to that friggin' hole in the ground.

Playing the grieving widow for television. Being a campaign prop for two assholes wanna be President. I'm through with it, I'm done. Sideshow over.

ALICE. That –

CHRISTA. I know, I know, it's hallowed grounds. To you. To me, it's just a friggin' hole in the ground. And if it was so friggin' hallowed, they would have built something there by now. It's just real estate at this point, pure and simple.

ALICE. That is where our husbands died.

CHRISTA. No. Our husbands died eight hundred feet in the air, not down in some shopping mall in the ground. You wanna visit where our husbands died, you gotta rent a helicopter. That hole in the ground bears as much resemblance to my husband as this bowl of lukewarm soup and at least this can be reheated. I'm tired, Alice, I'm just tired. I can't keep living my life as if it were the direct result of my husband's death. He died. He's dead. It doesn't make a difference how. Could have just as easily been a car crash or cancer, the result is just the same. Only with those, you don't have Presidential candidates showing up every four years on the anniversary of their death. It's the same thing, over and over and over. It doesn't mean anything any more. (*Off* ALICE*'s reaction.*) No, I'm sorry. I know it means something. It's just… what it doesn't mean any more is Peter. For me, at least. So I think I'm just going to surrender it to them: let the politicians make speeches in front of it, let CNN and Fox News sell ads while running stories about it, let the assholes sell their T-shirts outside Trinity church. I'm going to leave it to them and go find some other way to mark the occasion. Or maybe I won't mark it at all. Maybe that might be even better. But, whatever I do, I just can't do this any more.

ALICE. Don't you feel you owe it to Peter?

CHRISTA. I'm raising his daughters all by myself. I don't owe Peter anything.

Pause.

I'm sorry, I… I'm done.

5. September 11, 2007

ALICE, KELLY *and* CHRISTA.

KELLY. Every year around the end of August, without fail, I start craving blueberry pancakes. Like my internal clock telling me the anniversary is approaching. I only eat them on this one day of the year. It's so much nicer to think of it in those terms: my blueberry pancake day.

   Pause.

ALICE. It was a smaller service this year. I didn't see nearly as many of the old faces. Did you get this sense that so many of the people there didn't want to be there?

CHRISTA. It's not exactly something one does for fun.

ALICE. It just seemed, I don't know, such an afterthought. Like they were going through the motions. When I was in DC last week, testifying, I overheard a reporter say to another: 'God, here come the widows again. Don't these women have lives?' I turned to her and I said, 'I have a life. My life is to make sure people like you don't forget what happened because as soon as we do, it will happen again.'

CHRISTA. Well, not everyone carries it the way you do.

ALICE. How do I carry it?

CHRISTA. Like Atlas.

   Or Sisyphus.

   Silence.

KELLY. I'm moving to Oregon.

6. September 11, 2006

ALICE, KELLY *and* CHRISTA *eat silently.*

ALICE. I'm so happy we're all here this year.

KELLY. Yes.

ALICE. It's nice to be back. I don't ever want to… I regretted not being there last year. It was such a mistake.

CHRISTA. Don't do that to yourself.

ALICE. It was wrong not being here. There are fifty-one other weeks in the year.

CHRISTA. Don't beat yourself up. She beats herself up. You made a decision. A healthy decision. You went to Paris with your sister instead of this shitty little coffee shop. Brava, sweetie. Don't beat yourself up. Have a baguette and pretend you're there now.

ALICE. I'm here now.

KELLY. We're all here now.

ALICE. Yes.

Pause.

It's nice to be back.

7. September 11, 2005

The booth is empty. The WAITRESS *comes by and wipes it down, then moves along.*

8. September 11, 2004

KELLY *and* ALICE *are laughing at something.*

CHRISTA *clearly doesn't find it nearly as humorous.*

ALICE. He just flipped right over the hedge. No, actually, that's not true. He didn't. His bike did. He went right into the hedge. I have a picture at home – I'll email it to you – of the bike doing this somersault over the hedge and Charlie diving headfirst into the goddamned thing, his legs all akimbo, as if he was being sucked into some kind of a wormhole.

KELLY. I can't imagine Charlie on a bike.

ALICE. Well, he wasn't on it for long!

They die laughing.

KELLY. I'd never heard that story before. Christa, had you ever heard that story?

CHRISTA. I'd heard the story.

KELLY. I can just see Charlie getting sucked into that hedge.

ALICE. I'll send you the picture when I get home tonight.

KELLY. Charlie always – well, he was the kindest man / in the world.

ALICE. Thank you.

KELLY. But, I don't know, I think I always imagined him born in a suit.

ALICE. He took his work very seriously but I always made sure he didn't take himself too seriously.

KELLY. Steve worked all the time.

ALICE. That's what you do when you're Steve's age.

CHRISTA. Were.

ALICE. What?

CHRISTA. 'That's what you do when you were Steve's age.'

Silence.

KELLY. Anyway, Steve so admired Charlie.

(*To* CHRISTA.) Peter, too. He –

She starts to cry. ALICE *reaches a hand out to her and as she does, gives* CHRISTA *a death stare.* CHRISTA *looks out into space.*

CHRISTA. Work, work, work, that's all they ever talked about. Work or kids. Kids or work. You'd think to hear us we were the most boring group of people ever assembled. Maybe we were. Peter used to be at his desk every morning at 7:30 to catch his counterpart in London on the phone before he left for lunch. I told him, call him from home, be with your kids a little longer. But no. He had to be at his desk in the office with his papers. It had to happen properly. Couldn't call London from Brooklyn Heights, how unprofessional. Couldn't have the Brits hearing a four- and a seven-year-old running around, no, that just wouldn't do. You're lucky you and Steve never had kids, Kelly. I know it doesn't feel that way, but you are.

She finishes her drink, grabs her cigarettes.

I'll be right back.

She exits. Silence a moment.

9. September 11, 2003

ALICE, KELLY *and* CHRISTA. *A weight upon them. Great discomfort. They eat in silence.*

CHRISTA *starts to cry.* ALICE *reaches a hand out to her.*

10. September 11, 2002

ALICE, KELLY *and* CHRISTA. KELLY *peruses a menu.*
CHRISTA *drinks a whiskey. It is awkward and deeply raw.*

KELLY. I feel like pancakes. Blueberry pancakes, that's what I want.

She closes her menu, looks around, looks down. Silence.

That was beautiful. Wasn't it? Just / beautiful.

ALICE. It was. Very reverent and tasteful.

CHRISTA. I've been dreading this day for so long.

ALICE. Did you find any solace?

CHRISTA. I honestly hadn't been looking.

Silence.

KELLY. I can't believe it's been a year already. One whole year.

Silence.

ALICE. It's good we're doing this. This makes me glad. I wouldn't have wanted… anything else.

KELLY. We should do this every year. Make it our tradition.

ALICE. That would be nice.

The WAITRESS *enters,* KELLY *waves for her. She grabs her pad and crosses to them.*

WAITRESS. Yes, ladies… what can I get you?

11. September 16, 2000

Windows on the World. ALICE, CHRISTA *and* KELLY *enter.*

KELLY. Wow!

CHRISTA. I told you.

KELLY. I mean wow!

CHRISTA. Amazing, right? Look, you can see all the way to Weehawken. Those New Jerseans really have all the luck. They get views of Manhattan. We get views of New Jersey. How is that fair?

ALICE (*checking her watch*). They're late.

CHRISTA. They'll be here.

(*To* KELLY.) Mamma bear runs a tight ship.

(*To* ALICE.) Alice, calm yourself. Let go. Have a drink. They'll be here soon enough and then all the interesting conversation will end. Better fill up while you can.

KELLY. Thank you for taking me here.

ALICE. It's our pleasure. Every new member of the family – and that is how we think of everyone here – everyone is taken out to dinner after their very first day at work. Company tradition.

CHRISTA. But don't get too used to it. The other company tradition is that it'll also be the last time you ever get invited to dinner up here. The boys save this place for themselves. Always a quick drink upstairs before heading home. Or a breakfast meeting upstairs before work. They practically live up here. So your husband will be here all the time and the next meal you get on the company's dime will be at that shitty little coffee shop up the block. So take a good look now, kiddo.

ALICE. When Charlie told me they were leasing offices up here, I thought it was incredibly ostentatious. Great views can be greatly distracting. But they can also be greatly inspiring.

CHRISTA. So when you ask your husband why he never gets a raise, here's your answer. This view is his compensation. But you try putting two kids through private school with a view of the Hudson River.

ALICE. Christa.

CHRISTA. I've said my piece.

ALICE. We're happy to have you with us. It's very important to our husbands that we keep a strong family connection within the firm. It was started by my husband and his brother. Christa's husband started as an intern and learned everything he knows – which is quite a lot, I'll tell you – from them. And now your husband. It's important we maintain that family feel. I simply don't think the company would work without it.

KELLY. Thank you, I... thank you.

They all look out at the view.

What a gorgeous view of the harbor. Do you see how perfectly formed it is? That long, elegant curve? This was always going to be a great city, based solely on the shape of that harbor. It was inevitable. As if ordained by God. You'd have to try really hard to not make this city work.

CHRISTA. But boy, do they keep trying.

KELLY. The narrows, there. You see? Between Brooklyn and Staten Island? That's the key. It was so easy to protect. George Washington, I don't care what you say, was no great military genius. He didn't so much beat the British as just wait for them to get tired and go home.

They stare at her, not expecting such insight from her.

Oh. I'm kind of a history nerd. Didn't you watch the Ken Burns documentary? If it's worth knowing, Ken Burns has made a film about it.

They stare back out at the view.

That harbor made everything possible. It protected us from the rest of the world. We could build our city – and for that matter, our nation – completely undisturbed, isolated and safe. No one was ever getting in unless we wanted them to. How perfect. Everyone had to come in and go out through that one narrow channel. What better place to build a great city? How could we not succeed? What could ever happen to us here?

They continue to stare at the view.

End of play.

BROADCAST YOURSELF

Mona Mansour

126

Characters
CHORUS ONE
CHORUS TWO
CHORUS THREE
CHORUS FOUR
CHORUS FIVE
CHORUS SIX
CHORUS SEVEN
CHORUS EIGHT

The List

CHORUS ONE. Every single day, at some point in the day, I watch a different one. It's just become part of my routine. You do this, and you get to know which ones are best.

Never Before Seen Video of WTC 9/11 Attack, by JmanFIVEk, has over eighteen million views. It's exactly what it says it is: never before seen video of the World Trade Center attack. I appreciate that. And it's fifty seconds long. Perfect if I'm at work and don't want someone walking by to really know what I'm looking at. Well. I mean. It's not porn but it's not work-related, so –

CHORUS TWO. When you type '9-11 people', in the search window, what

immediately pops up is:

'people jumping out,' 'people running,' and just 'people,'

In that order.

CHORUS ONE. Which tells me that the main thing people want to see is

people jumping out, first. Which, if I'm being honest, is

what *I* want to see, first.

CHORUS TWO. Not the moment of impact. It's not that. It's the fall,

somehow. The drop. Something about what it is right before

someone dies. What do they look like right before they die?

CHORUS THREE. Other videos:

CHORUS FOUR. **World Trade Center Attacks,** by tributes4wtc

CHORUS ONE. Pretty standard. Nothing earth-shattering, footage-wise. But it should be on the list. If I had a list. I mean, if I wrote it down. I'm not that obsessive.

CHORUS FIVE. **En la terraza del World Trade Center: On the rooftop of the**

World Trade Center. by SergioMZA, just under three million views.

CHORUS TWO. See, that title? That's a bad title. Misleading. You think it's going to be ON THE DAY. Can you imagine? Footage from the roof, on the day? That would be – but no, it's just a day up there. Some random other day. Still, with a title like that, you'd think there'd be more views.

CHORUS FIVE. What is a view? If I watch it six times, does that count as six views?

CHORUS THREE. **9/11: Total Proof that Bombs Were Planted in the Buildings!** by NuffRespect.

CHORUS ONE. The top comment: mclmatty, from one day ago:

CHORUS FOUR. God Bless You.

CHORUS TWO. The second top comment, from two days ago:

CHORUS SIX. 'LADIES AND GENTLEMEN: 1. The Holocaust against the Jews did NOT happen on the scale we are led to believe. 2. Israel did 9/11 so that the racist West could start bashing and occupying Muslim countries.' – Investigator.

CHORUS ONE. And the most recent comment, one hour ago:

CHORUS SEVEN. 'Hawt,' and 'I also needed a tissue box. I spunked everywhere,'

CHORUS ONE. Both from killuminati87.

CHORUS SEVEN. My favourite? If I had to pick. I mean, just one: Is called

September 11, 2001 video, Posted by Net WorkLive. At the beginning of it, these words roll:

CHORUS FOUR. Five years ago, we watched and filmed the attack on the WTC out of the window of our home, thirty-six floors up and five hundred yards away from the North Towers. Releasing this tape was a difficult decision for us because of its emotional and personal nature, and the potential for misuse. We feel, however, that our unique perspective has an important historical value, and shows the horror of the day without soundtracks or hype found in other accounts.

CHORUS ONE. Blah blah blah blah blah.

CHORUS TWO. Bob and Bri, 9/11, 2006.

CHORUS EIGHT. It starts off. You're looking out the window. The first tower is already smoking. It's quiet. Bree – she says it like that – Bree has got music on in the background.

CHORUS FOUR. What song is playing?

CHORUS EIGHT. I can't tell. I've tried to figure it out. A kid's song. I think it's a kid's song. Well anyway, Bob and Bri have a kid. Lily. You hear later, when the towers are falling, you hear the mom, Bri, say,

CHORUS FIVE. 'Hold Lily! Hold Lily!'

CHORUS EIGHT. Like somehow that's the thing to do in that moment. The first few minutes are just Bri and the song, and the tower, and it's pretty calm. Then something amazing happens: Bri opens the window. Her window. And suddenly, the whole thing changes. The whole thing.

CHORUS FOUR. The window opens: Sirens. Smoke. You can't hear smoke, but still. Suddenly it's all LOUD

CHORUS ONE. And it's like THAT'S IT. It's happening.

CHORUS EIGHT. Bri's voice changes. She scream-talks. Scream-talks the rest of the time. You hear her husband say

CHORUS SIX. They're attacking the World Trade Center, not us.

CHORUS FOUR. Which I guess is supposed to be comforting, even though the World Trade Center is directly across the street from these people. I guess you say things at times like that. Whether they make sense or not.

CHORUS EIGHT. When the first one collapses, Bri starts crying like a baby. And Bob says,

CHORUS SIX. We're okay, we're okay.

CHORUS TWO. Then it cuts to that huge smoke column in the streets, it's oozing towards them.

CHORUS EIGHT. And Bri says,

CHORUS FIVE. Oh my God, all those people down there. Do you think we're okay?

CHORUS EIGHT. And he says,

CHORUS SIX. I think we're okay, I think we're okay.

CHORUS EIGHT. 'Think.' Now he just 'thinks'.

CHORUS SEVEN. It's not the most viewed 9/11 video. Not by far. Only nine nine hundred and twenty thousand, a hundred and forty-eight hits

CHORUS ONE. **Satans's face seen in WTC Plane Crash Explosion,** stickybomb, has 2 million more

CHORUS EIGHT. Really? Satan's face in the Twin Towers? Do you need to see Satan's face? Isn't it horrific enough already? All of it?

THE CHILDREN

DC Moore

132

Characters

AYESHA, *late twenties, Pakistani but was educated overseas so has an accent which sometimes hovers over the Atlantic*

JASON, *around thirty, American*

HOSPITAL PORTERS/DOCTORS/NURSES/PATIENTS, *any age, gender, Pakistani*

A hospital waiting room, Karachi. AYESHA is stood against a wall, away from JASON, who is sat nursing a coffee. JASON's hand has had some stitching over a nasty cut. There is a fairly decrepit vending machine near them.

A bloody PATIENT is rushed through the room on a trolley/gurney by a few Urdu-speaking PORTERS/NURSES/DOCTORS (in the rush it may not be clear which is which), shouting things like 'Jaldi Karo' ['hurry up']. A rush of voices, then silence.

A pause.

AYESHA. She asked for this.

JASON *shrugs. Exhales.*

I wish I smoked, sometimes.

JASON. Yeah.

AYESHA. You know?

JASON. Yeah.

AYESHA. For waiting. Time.

JASON. I know, yeah. To pass the…

AYESHA *nods.*

JASON *nods.*

A pause.

AYESHA. Have you ever smoked?

JASON. Nope.

AYESHA. What about, weed?

JASON *gives her a look.*

JASON. A little.

AYESHA. At college?

JASON. Where else?

AYESHA. Me too.

JASON *nods*.

A brief pause.

JASON. I was in my dorm. Stoned as a… Watching TV. When the second plane…

JASON *does a little gesture to suggest the plane's movement/impact.*

AYESHA *nods*.

A fluorescent light is flickering on and off. AYESHA *looks up at the light.* JASON *watches her.* AYESHA *notices her watching him.*

AYESHA. You don't have to, to stay.

JASON. I'm here.

AYESHA. I know but…

JASON. At least till we find out how they both are.

AYESHA. Okay. And are you… okay?

JASON. Yeah. Me? Yeah.

A pause.

AYESHA. Are you armed?

JASON. What?

AYESHA. Are you? Now?

A brief pause.

JASON *nods*.

Good. Have you used it? Since you got here?

JASON. Ayesha.

AYESHA. What?

JASON. I'm not…

AYESHA. What?

JASON. You're being… quite… fucking…

AYESHA. I don't know what you're…?

JASON. She asked for it?

AYESHA. She practically arranged it.

JASON. You are very...

AYESHA. What?

JASON. I just don't... I don't understand you.

JASON *fidgets with his coffee cup. Taps it repeatedly.*

Nobody asks to die like that.

AYESHA. Of course they do.

JASON. No.

AYESHA. Every day.

JASON. Not like that.

AYESHA. Yes.

JASON.... Okay. Okay. *Fine.*

A brief pause.

AYESHA. Are you angry with me?

JASON. *Yes.*

AYESHA. Why?

JASON. Because you are so... fucking...

AYESHA. What?

JASON....

AYESHA. What, Jason?

JASON.... *cold.*

AYESHA. Yes. I have to be.

JASON. Really?

AYESHA *nods.*

Jesus. Because it seems like. To me. Sometimes. It seems like it's a fucking. A choice. To be like this.

AYESHA *smiles a little.*

AYESHA. You're being righteous.

JASON. Yes, yes I am.

AYESHA. My second favourite.

JASON. What?

AYESHA. Of the ways you are.

A brief pause.

JASON. Ayesha.

AYESHA. What?

JASON. Don't. Not, not here.

AYESHA. Okay.

JASON nods, looks away from her.

JASON. This fucking city.

AYESHA. Yes.

JASON (*with a hint of a smile*). I think Karachi is literally how I imagine Hell.

AYESHA nods. Also a hint of a smile.

AYESHA. What does that make me?

JASON (*not malicious, honest*). I... I don't really know.

A brief pause.

AYESHA (*referring to his hand/stitches*). Does it hurt?

JASON shakes his head.

A brief pause.

JASON. She was trying to help people, that's all. By standing. Saying, I can lead this country. I can take it back. She was. She was trying to help all those... All those... All those... All those... fucking... people. You know?

AYESHA. No.

JASON. She was, in my... Yeah. That's what I think. She didn't *ask* for *this*.

AYESHA. Saving them?

JASON. Yes.

AYESHA. From what?

JASON. An absence.

AYESHA. Of…?

JASON. … *anything*. Rights. Order. Fucking. *Logic*.

AYESHA (*softly*). The way you curse.

JASON. Ayesha. My point is… My fucking point… is…

A brief pause.

Okay, I don't have a point. I don't know. I just don't see how you can see another Bhutto – family – die like that – today – and be like this, now.

AYESHA. She isn't the first I've lost.

JASON. Yeah… I know. You just seem so…

AYESHA. Ready?

JASON. Yeah.

AYESHA. That isn't my fault. Every year, we lose another. There's just three of us, now.

JASON. Yeah. Yeah, I know.

A pause.

I haven't had to use it. Not yet.

AYESHA. What?

JASON gestures very vaguely to his weapon.

JASON. And I don't want to. But I would.

Another bloody PATIENT is rushed through the room on a trolley/gurney by HOSPITAL PORTERS/DOCTORS/NURSES – more shouting/barking of orders. Maybe more hellish/bloody than the previous PATIENT.

JASON watches them go. Takes out a phone.

Two bombers, according to Reuters. Fifty-eight dead now.

AYESHA nods.

AYESHA. But it could be sixty.

JASON. … yeah.

A brief pause.

Did you get to see them at all, before I found you?

AYESHA *shakes her head.*

AYESHA. In the panic, I… No. They were too far, from me.

JASON. How old are they?

AYESHA. Eight and five.

JASON. Fuck. And doesn't that…? You are so…

AYESHA. I won't cry again, Jason.

JASON. Okay, but…

AYESHA. I won't. I promised myself.

JASON. Your cousins.

AYESHA. Yes.

JASON. Your own…

AYESHA. Yes. This happens. When you stand in an open place – in Karachi, of all… – and tell people you are theirs. They claim you back.

JASON *shakes his head.*

She asked for this.

JASON. Fine. Fine.

A brief pause.

JASON *is inspecting his wound/stitching.*

AYESHA. Will it scar?

JASON *nods.*

Memento.

JASON *nods.*

A pause.

Have you called your, your parents?

JASON. What?

AYESHA. They'll see the news. They'll worry.

JASON. No.

AYESHA. Of course they will.

JASON shakes his head.

JASON. I told them that I was – that I am – stationed in Germany. Diplomatic service, so. What do they know. I only ever email them on my personal account: it's easy enough. Google Berlin daylife, cut and paste. Mix in some reality to…

AYESHA. I like that.

JASON. They wouldn't even want me drinking the water here, let alone…

A brief pause.

AYESHA. Is there a German me?

JASON. Fuck.

AYESHA. Really? There is?

A brief pause.

JASON. Maria.

AYESHA. That's my name?

JASON nods.

I like it.

JASON. Yeah.

AYESHA. What have you said about me?

JASON. Just that I…

AYESHA. What?

JASON.… that I met someone.

AYESHA. Maria.

JASON. Yeah. Stupid.

AYESHA. No. I like it. Is there a photo, of her?

JASON. Not yet.

AYESHA. Will there be?

JASON. We'll see.

AYESHA. Copy me in, when.

JASON. Okay. But she'll be fat. And bald.

AYESHA. Okay.

JASON. And Swiss.

AYESHA. Not a local?

JASON shakes his head.

JASON. Not at all. And she'll be. Cold. From all those years growing up, in the fucking. In the Alps. So. Acclimatised. She will be. That whatever she touches. Dies.

AYESHA. Jay.

JASON. From the lack of. Of heat. Yeah, I'll make sure I copy you in.

AYESHA nods.

AYESHA. Thank you.

A pause.

JASON. You don't think that she was trying to help?

AYESHA shakes his head.

AYESHA. She just wanted Pakistan to play with again. To hang around with your ambassadors and tell them everything was being solved. That it's all. Simple.

JASON. Elections. A voice. Change.

AYESHA shakes her head.

AYESHA. Toys.

JASON. I think you're too close, to see it.

AYESHA. I know you do.

JASON. I can see it.

AYESHA. I know you can.

JASON. I can.

AYESHA. Yes.

A pause.

JASON. What are their names?

AYESHA. Amir and Jia.

JASON *nods.*

JASON. Right. Which is younger?

AYESHA. Amir.

JASON. Okay. Jia is eight. Amir is five.

AYESHA. Yes.

JASON *nods.*

A DOCTOR *enters, smoking. He ambles over to the vending machine. En route he stares at* JASON, *with an edge of unease. Gets to the vending machine, enters coins. As the machine serves him a coffee, he stares at* AYESHA, *exhales a little smoke in her direction. Shakes his head a little. He then goes.*

JASON. They're gonna need me back in Islamabad.

AYESHA. Why?

JASON. To assess the political… whatever, of all this.

JASON *motions to his cut/bandage.*

This buys me some time. But not much.

AYESHA. And what are they?

JASON. What?

AYESHA. The political whatever.

JASON. You know.

AYESHA. Tell me.

A pause.

JASON. The normal. Another win for militants. Talibanisation. The ongoing death of secular politics. The death of… all of it. But everyone in Washington has actually heard of… Benazir. And the Bhuttos. Even you. The niece. So they'll read the reports this time.

A brief pause.

And as well we'll have to make nods at our own security. Use less locals, tighten… whatever. We're getting fairly used to all this now. There are motions to go through. Tedious, mainly.

AYESHA. You wish you were writing about trade talks in Berlin.

JASON. Maybe.

AYESHA. Economic tariffs and GDPs.

JASON. It's what I studied, what I know, but…

AYESHA. … you need to be here?

JASON *nods*.

I'm nearly glad you are.

JASON. What?

AYESHA. Here.

A brief pause.

A DOCTOR *enters, who is clearly known to both* AYESHA *and* JASON.

DOCTOR. I have some news.

Blackout.

SUPERMAN

Abi Morgan

Characters

EDITOR, *early/mid-thirties*

ACTRESS, *late twenties*

INTERN

JOURNALIST

SPIN DOCTOR

SECRETARY

REALITY STAR

Plus INTERNS, JOURNALISTS, SECRETARIES *and* SUB-EDITORS

Scene 1

The EDITOR *and the* ACTRESS.

An office, Canary Wharf, London, September 2001.

The EDITOR *sits across a desk from* ACTRESS.

The bell and whistles of a newsroom beyond, underscore.

EDITOR. And what day was this?

ACTRESS. Friday.

EDITOR. Again at the Radisson?

ACTRESS. It's near and he needs to be there early. Depending on what time the match kicks off.

An INTERN *enters, slides a series of mock-ups down on the* EDITOR*'s desk.*

EDITOR. Right. Convenient.

The EDITOR *peers down at them, distracted. The* INTERN *hovers.*

ACTRESS. Cheap.

EDITOR. I didn't say that.

The EDITOR *taps a mock-up on his desk, nods to the* INTERN.

Okay none of these are right, tell him to start again, I don't like repeating myself.

The INTERN *makes to exit. The phone rings.*

Figures in yet?

INTERN. Kerry's going to patch them through.

The EDITOR *nods.*

EDITOR. Let's just top the fucking *Sun* eh?

Forgive me.

The ACTRESS *shrugs, smiles.*

ACTRESS. Of course.

EDITOR. So, Roger sends me lots of people. Why us? We've not met before.

ACTRESS. I feel as if we have.

EDITOR. I'll need dates.

ACTRESS. May 4th. Charity match.

Suddenly the ACTRESS *is distracted, watching a plane pass by –*

Christ –

EDITOR. City Airport. They were grounded all day yesterday but –

The EDITOR *watches the plane passing overhead.*

… the morning after, life goes on.

The ACTRESS *smiles. The* EDITOR *smiles.*

Was he on his own?

ACTRESS. No. The whole family was with him… Not his youngest… She wasn't there but the boys were and I had a very nice conversation with his wife –

EDITOR. Annie.

ACTRESS. They've –

EDITOR. …. been together a long time.

ACTRESS. Which makes it very difficult for him to leave her.

JOURNALIST. *Tinkerbell!*

EDITOR. Yeah.

JOURNALIST. Mike's line 2. Kerry's patching him through.

The EDITOR *nods, stands, distracted, peering out of the window to the street far below.*

EDITOR. Did you speak to him?

ACTRESS. Just chit-chat. He was flirting… She took the boys home early…

EDITOR. And that's when it happened.

ACTRESS. Not that night. It wasn't tacky… We had dinner. This is killing him…

EDITOR. I'm sure.

ACTRESS. Not least because of the children…

The phone rings. The EDITOR *snatches up the telephone.*

EDITOR. Yep… Mike… Get on with it cunt. Break it to me… Fucking marvellous…

INTERN. How much?

The EDITOR *gestures to the clutch of* INTERNS, JOURNALISTS, SECRETARIES *and* SUB-EDITORS *seated beyond, or hovering in a doorway.*

EDITOR. How much? Through the fucking roof.

A resounding cheer goes up.

Up 400,000.

A bigger cheer.

You are a gentleman and a scholar… We did… we wiped the fucking floor with them… Yep… Yep… Indeed cunt of the highest order… Love to Bruce.

The EDITOR *slams down the phone.*

Out!

The INTERN *exits. The* EDITOR *sits, then stands barely able to contain himself.*

Yesterday's sales.

The ACTRESS *nods. The* EDITOR *whoops, barely able to contain himself, throwing a smile to a passing colleague. The* EDITOR *pokes his head out.*

(*Calling after.*) Send Rebekah a magnum of champagne. Tell her to shove it where the *Sun* doesn't shine.

ACTRESS. Congratulations.

EDITOR. Interestingly only half of what we got on Diana.

ACTRESS. Really.

EDITOR. Sorry. You were having dinner?

The ACTRESS *hesitates, resumes.*

ACTRESS (*nods*). He said he just knew as soon as he saw me.

I was very raw after the divorce.

EDITOR. We did warn you.

ACTRESS. You did. You did.

EDITOR. *Run for your life!*

ACTRESS. That was a horrible cartoon.

EDITOR. He was a fucking footballer what did you expect, sweetheart.

Laughter –

ACTRESS. I know. I know.

A JOURNALIST *passes by, raising a thumbs-up to the* EDITOR. *He smiles, throws him a lewd gesture of delight, laughing as the* JOURNALIST *moves on.*

EDITOR. And they have a photo?

ACTRESS. It's nothing. He's just getting into a bloody car and I peck him on the cheek.

EDITOR. You love him.

ACTRESS. Cynic.

EDITOR. Not at all. I'm a big fan of love.

Laughter.

Really.

ACTRESS. Stop it.

The EDITOR *smiles. The* ACTRESS *smiles.*

EDITOR. So if I call him he won't deny it? They'll perceive you as a home-wrecker.

ACTRESS. I'm not.

They're going to run it whatever. So if it's going to be out there I want you to break it.

EDITOR. Thank you.

ACTRESS. No really. I trust you. The coverage these last few days.

EDITOR. Yes.

ACTRESS. Honestly I don't know how you do it. How any of you do it?

EDITOR. Yes.

ACTRESS. Neither of us could sleep. We had the TV on all day. We just clung to one another, watching.

The EDITOR, *already moving on, looking back at the pages on his desk.*

If he loved her, don't you think he would have been with her that night. No seriously. Seriously.

ACTRESS. Love is all we have.

The whir of the newsroom all around.

Scene 2

The EDITOR, *the* INTERN *and the* JOURNALIST.

Late.

Five days later.

JOURNALIST. He's out of control.

The JOURNALIST *and the* INTERN *pore over a series of headline mock-ups across the desk.*

INTERN. He thinks he's John Wayne.

The EDITOR *peers out of the window.*

EDITOR. We should all have parachutes.

JOURNALIST. Eh?

EDITOR. I'm serious. £500 a pop army surplus.

JOURNALIST. I'd rather fry. Grab the nearest bottle, lock myself in the gents with Tits Marie and bang my way to oblivion, thank you.

EDITOR. While I will land like Colonel Blimp, coffee in hand.

The EDITOR *drinks, peers at a variety of photos of 9/11 on his wall and desk.*

Why was there so little blood? Look at it. Simple, disintegration.

Total white-out. What are the other tossers leading with?

JOURNALIST. Bush the Trigger-Happy Texan; Laden, Head on a Platter –

The JOURNALIST *picks up a copy of the* Sun, *holding up the headline: 'Are we at War? Absolutely.'*

And Are We at War? Absolutely.

EDITOR. We're not here to serve the Government, we're here to serve the readers. Let 'em suck up to Downing Street, we err on caution. Bush is playing to absolute type and Blair is desperate to keep up, boys who want to be heroes for a day.

The EDITOR *points at a photograph.*

You want to know who the real heroes are? This guy. This guy. Not the politicians and the generals. Real people died, this was democratic, it was everyone from the top floor down.

JOURNALIST. Did you read Johnny's piece?

EDITOR. Fucking –

JOURNALIST. Brilliant.

EDITOR. Pair of tits I would fuck that ugly genius.

JOURNALIST. Twice. Once because I could. Twice because I would fuck –

EDITOR. …. that mind.

JOURNALIST. That mind.

EDITOR. He's fucking Dostoevsky.

JOURNALIST. I cried.

EDITOR. Exactly. People need a chink of light, they need hope. Let's lift them from the rubble, get Michael to find this guy. If he's still alive? Let's find out, let's get an interview.

JOURNALIST. And put him where?

EDITOR. Ahh… bump Duncan Smith and put him on five.

The JOURNALIST *nods, makes to go –*

What do you think about parachutes?

JOURNALIST. Eh?

EDITOR. We're on the thirtieth floor, we get hit, and what do you have then?

The JOURNALIST *exits. The* EDITOR *peers up, eyes following a plane travelling overhead, craning to watch as it passes, just out of view until –*

What?

The INTERN *hovers in the door.*

INTERN. She's on the phone again.

The EDITOR *hesitates, nods.*

What should I say?

EDITOR. I'm out.

The INTERN *makes to go.*

Would you jump or fry?

The INTERN *looks at him nonplussed. The* EDITOR *picks up a photo and peers at it.*

Tell Robbie to hold the front page.

Find me this Superman.

Scene 3

The office.

The EDITOR *and the* SPIN DOCTOR *stand facing one another. The* SPIN DOCTOR *holds up a* Mirror *newspaper page that reads 'THIS WAR'S A FRAUD'.*

SPIN DOCTOR. THIS WAR'S A FRAUD! What the fuck are you doing?

EDITOR. I could ask you the same thing. To what do I owe this pleasure?

SPIN DOCTOR. Piss off.

EDITOR. Speaks well. I'd fuck him. But he won't save the world.

SPIN DOCTOR. Someone has to.

EDITOR. Can I quote you on that?

SPIN DOCTOR. Are we a sceptic?

EDITOR. Not at all, play it right and he'll win you another term, but he's easily led. That's why you're there.

A SECRETARY *hovers by a door. The* EDITOR *gestures for her to go away.*

Silence.

SPIN DOCTOR. When Bush is pulling on the leash to go for Saddam, I hope we can count on you when we're trying to hold him back.

EDITOR. Yes you can, if you do.

The ring of distant phones. JOURNALISTS *peering across their desks, beyond curious.*

But from where I'm standing it looks like we're bombing the life out of a pile of rubble, smashing a lot of rocks to find Bin Laden in a city he's not hiding in by the way, and killing innocent civilians.

SPIN DOCTOR. It's selling your papers.

EDITOR. Us questioning it is what's selling papers.

SPIN DOCTOR. Not *Big Brother*?! Your radical crusading newspaper! Betty from Birmingham! The hot tub!

EDITOR. And what does it say on the front?

What's wrong? Nervous?

The EDITOR *smiles. The* SPIN DOCTOR *shrugs.*

SPIN DOCTOR. I just question what you will be remembered for.

EDITOR. Delivering extraordinary news in extraordinary times.

SPIN DOCTOR. Oh, that's what your boys found rifling through my bins.

EDITOR. Not mine.

The SPIN DOCTOR *wavers, smiles makes to go.*

SPIN DOCTOR. Nice to know who your friends are. I thought we were.

EDITOR. Interesting. Past tense.

The SPIN DOCTOR *hesitates.*

You know Betty from Birmingham might just have something to talk about now she's out. For once Betties everywhere are talking about anthrax and Al-Qaeda rather than who's fucking who in *Corrie*. We've done that.

SPIN DOCTOR. Why are you doing this? You're not a Tory paper. We're in the middle of fucking open-heart surgery, trying to remove a tumour, and you think you can scrub up and smart-arse from across the operating theatre.

EDITOR. What do you want me to do, mop your brow? I know how complicated this is for you, but I really believe the public want to understand.

SPIN DOCTOR. You're asking me to trust you.

EDITOR. Why not?

SPIN DOCTOR. On matters of international security?

EDITOR. Think of us as your conscience.

SPIN DOCTOR. You lure the public in with smutty revelations of reality stars then once you've got them you whip up the moral majority to suspect everything we do.

EDITOR. We serve a hungry public who want Bin Laden caught as much as you do. We're just questioning your methods of doing so.

SPIN DOCTOR. You're warping public opinion and punching above your weight. At least let the bloody public hear what we have to say.

EDITOR. We are gauging the temperature of the public –

SPIN DOCTOR. You are setting that temperature. You give us signs of support –

EDITOR. We do.

SPIN DOCTOR.... then kick us in the nuts with sensationalist headline –

EDITOR. If you deserve it.

Have you found any weapons of mass destruction?

Silence.

Have you?

Silence.

Thought not. Good luck with Bin Laden.

A JOURNALIST *passes. The* SPIN DOCTOR *nods, smiles, waits until he passes, moving in close on the* EDITOR.

SPIN DOCTOR. This moment in the sun, it too will pass. When we capture Bin Laden and we will, your newspaper will be the first to put the photos of him paraded in front of a vengeful public on your front page. And then you will go back to doing what you do best. Digging around in dustbins and eavesdropping into the lives of the bereft and the famous and destroying the innocent. That's what you'll be remembered for.

The EDITOR *smiles, holds his ground.*

EDITOR. I won't be alone then.

The incessant ring of a distant phone.

Scene 4

Dawn.

The office.

The EDITOR *enters his office, he hesitates with surprise, a* REALITY STAR *stands peering out of a window. Her hair is up in rollers.*

REALITY STAR. They put me in here.

The EDITOR *checks his watch, ignores her, heading to his desk, takeaway coffee in hand.*

EDITOR. Right. You are –

The REALITY STAR *smiles, nods.*

REALITY STAR. *Big Brother* 2.

EDITOR. Okay.

The EDITOR *goes through the pile of newspapers.*

REALITY STAR. Photo shoot. For the magazine.

The INTERN *enters –*

INTERN. Sorry, sorry. I didn't think anyone would be in this early.

EDITOR. Yeah, well they are.

INTERN. They're ready for you.

REALITY STAR. Thanks. I love your newspaper.

EDITOR. That's very sweet of you.

The REALITY STAR *exits.*

INTERN. Congratulations.

The EDITOR *nods, clearly hungover, wanting to be left alone.*

Must have been some party.

EDITOR. It was. What's she in for?

INTERN. *Stars in Spas.* They're all coming in today for a shoot. New reality show. Stars working in Spas.

EDITOR. Brilliant. And we're paying for this?

INTERN. Exclusive interview and a weekly column.

EDITOR. Who's writing it?

INTERN. 'She is.' It'll just be gossip and stuff.

EDITOR. Can't wait.

INTERN. Rob's laid out Monday's mock-up.

EDITOR. Bit early.

The EDITOR *smiles, holds up a mock-up of the* Mirror. *'Newspaper of the Year' bannered in the corner.*

Newspaper of the Year.

The EDITOR *looks up.*

Hello you.

The ACTRESS *stands in tracksuit, coffee, cellphone and a pack of cigarettes in hand, hair also in rollers.*

INTERN. Okay?

ACTRESS. Yes. They're just setting up the next shot.

INTERN. I'll come and get you. You in your swimwear.

ACTRESS. Yes.

The INTERN *nods, heads out.*

EDITOR. Don't tell me. You're in charge of waxing.

ACTRESS. For £50,000 I'll be in charge of anything. Good night?

EDITOR. It was rather.

ACTRESS. I called you –

EDITOR. Yes –

ACTRESS. For six weeks I called you.

EDITOR. You look wonderful. Sorry to hear that it didn't work out with –

ACTRESS. I finished it.

EDITOR. Good for you.

ACTRESS. You were just meant to bloody out him.

EDITOR. A different week and I may just have…

ACTRESS. Right.

EDITOR. Don't be like that. He didn't want to leave his wife.

The ACTRESS *laughs.*

He's a pal. I went to their wedding.

The EDITOR *smiles, drinks his coffee.*

ACTRESS. You're a parasite you know that.

EDITOR. They toasted us in Cristal last night, for our coverage of 9/11. Newspaper of the Year.

ACTRESS. Congratulations.

EDITOR. They come in once in a lifetime those stories, twice if you're lucky.

ACTRESS. Have you even slept?

EDITOR. Not a wink. Never do these days.

ACTRESS. You should cut out the coffee.

EDITOR. Now where's the fun in that.

ACTRESS. I'm seeing someone else now.

EDITOR. Well give us a call if you're offering an exclusive on that.

ACTRESS. You know you fuck people's lives up.

EDITOR. No, you do that yourself, darling.

ACTRESS. I wanted you to run it with some dignity.

EDITOR. It was an affair, not much dignity in that.

We knew about it months ago, and we got a better bloody photo.

The ACTRESS *reels.*

I wouldn't be doing my job if I didn't keep tabs.

ACTRESS. Who do you think you are?

EDITOR. I am the editor of the biggest-selling tabloid in the country. What about you?

ACTRESS. You know next time, when it happens next time, I hope it's a bloody big bomb and Fleet Street's its epicentre. I hope they kill the whole bloody lot of you. I don't know how you live with yourself.

EDITOR. Easily. I write my own lines and on the whole I choose whose cock is in my mouth. Not sure you can say the same sweetheart.

The ACTRESS *nods, exits. The* EDITOR *resumes drinking his coffee. Suddenly a phone rings. The* EDITOR *looks down, spies a cellphone on the desk. He picks it up. It rings off. He considers it. Suddenly the* ACTRESS *enters.*

Careful.

The ACTRESS *snatches the phone out of the* EDITOR's *hand.*

The EDITOR, *watching a plane passing overhead.*

The End.

TRIO WITH ACCOMPANIMENT

Rory Mullarkey

Characters

TUBE, *female*

PLANE, *male*

BUS, *female*

ANNOUNCEMENTS, *which may be performed by any number of actors*

Note on the Text

The effect should be polyphonic: as musical as it is dramatic.

The tempo is fairly brisk throughout, building towards the end.

TUBE. I think this is the loneliest place in the world

— Please mind the

— Welcome aboard your

— This station is

PLANE. God wish they'd out the way coz trying to get to my

— Calling at

BUS. Crowded today should have walked down to the next

— Stops to

— Doors closing

— Please store items in the overhead

TUBE. Today I think particularly it's the loneliest place

PLANE. Right on the wing yeah window seat for me

— 41 to

BUS. Top deck always go top deck bottom deck's for

TUBE. Purposefully boarding at the rear of the train

BUS. Little kids and old people

PLANE. Seatbelt on as soon as I sit down may as well you know metal tip in the buckle

TUBE. But it is still the loneliest place in the world I think

BUS. Top deck's drunks and rudeboys though

— This is your captain speaking

TUBE. Standing and swaying against one another I've rarely been so close

BUS. One free next to him one next to her him yeah him go near the button

PLANE. Always annoying muzak or some you know fucking Bach something like

TUBE. In many ways never been so close

BUS. Shit accidentally touched that guy's in the sitting down there

— Where the local time will be

PLANE. Hate this bit runway suddenly gets fast hate this

TUBE. But down here in the bowels of the earth and in the artificial

PLANE. Light switched on open up the air-conditioner cool down

BUS. Shouldn't have touched that there shit don't make eye contact

— Stand clear

— Mind the

TUBE. When I'm looking around people look at me

PLANE. Not in the mood for a chat mate not in the mood

— Crystal Palace Parade

TUBE. Chastised for having locked eyes with

— Mind the

BUS. Yeah but seriously move up a bit how big's your bum Jesus

ALL. Don't make eye contact

— There will now be a short safety

TUBE. Some stranger some other some unknown

PLANE. Don't make eye contact

TUBE. Some some

BUS. Don't make eye contact

TUBE. Just some fellow commuter I don't even know who you are

BUS. Not a long journey in terms of miles though the traffic though

PLANE. Shit though I mean just a floating metal tube

— No standing on the upper

— Please switch off all

BUS. Fucking actually amazed that it actually takes less time to get
   to a different country than just across the city

TUBE. But it could be any of us yes

PLANE. I mean what if we or someone

TUBE. In the event of the event

— All hand baggage stowed

— West Green Road

BUS. At least it's not night I fucking hate this journey at night is that guy looking at me talking all loud to his

PLANE. It would be well easy I mean I know there's all the security measures

TUBE. In the event of the event it could be any of us

BUS. So loud know what I mean

— There are six exits

PLANE. A guy once went for the cockpit they had to restrain

BUS. I mean I wish they'd keep it down in my country talk my language Jesus

TUBE. Like on any other day I am vigilantly looking out for potential suspects

PLANE. Ram-packed with air marshals I'd hope today transatlantic I mean reckon I could take them though you know

BUS. There's a smell to them they could have anything under

PLANE. Maybe not if I was outnumbered

— Seven Sisters Station

TUBE. In flowing clothing or fiddling with minimal dexterity with a new-looking rucksack

PLANE. Because in the shoes didn't one guy have actually underwear too imagine in your boxers having

— Please stand clear

ALL. Keep my eyes open

— 41 to

BUS. I mean they know it worries us don't they if they talk like that so loud one man the other day top deck faced Mecca and

PLANE. Suppose you can't check to see if they have a pilot's licence or

TUBE. I look around like I might look for someone I recognise

BUS. Enjoy that do they enjoy that we're scared of them

PLANE. If they bought a one-way ticket in cash

— Battersea Bridge Road

— A detachable slide will extend

— Mind the

TUBE. That's why always the rear of the train because they'd take the front wouldn't they or avoiding large crowds of people because obviously they'd intend on maximising the

PLANE. Couldn't light the fuse though because he'd been walking around in them all day

BUS. Because one of those that was on a bus wasn't it

PLANE. Lockerbie yes that was a though they crash more often than blown up don't they

BUS. How many of them died just as many as us coz multicultural

TUBE. Apparently it is a blinding white light and more like a pop than a bang and then obviously the light goes in the bowels of

— There are six emergency

PLANE. If you're so high up you're dead anyway doesn't matter if it's you know engine failure or

TUBE. A whooshing sound like everything expanding and contracting suddenly

BUS. A hole in the side sucking everything through

— Is located under the seat in front of you

TUBE. Then that darkness in the bowels of

BUS. Multiple nationalities scattered all over the square

TUBE. So maybe it would be better to push myself against another allow the force and shock of it to crush my organs entirely

PLANE. Hostesses they wouldn't even look at me only in movies guys actually manage with hostesses the Dutch ones I like the Dutch ones from the Hague maybe best think one of them easier to

— N3 to

— Slip the life vest over your head

PLANE. I would wreck her though I would destroy her it would be the time of her

— Life vests should remain stowed

— We are now at

BUS. Top deck to the road in one fell swoop

TUBE. Rather than waking up bleeding in that darkness in the bowels of

PLANE. If I stopped a terror threat though then she'd definitely fuck me

TUBE. And looking around wondering if any of these people would help me to get out alive

— Do make sure your own oxygen mask is correctly fitted before helping anyone else

BUS. None of these bastards even give a shit

PLANE. And I don't even know if had to make one of those phone calls who I'd call

TUBE. My legs turned to soup and unable to hear in my right ear

— An inflight meal

TUBE. Unable to

— Stand clear

TUBE. Unable to

— Move down

TUBE. Going out of my

— Mind the gap

— Croxted Road

— This train is for

TUBE. Wondering if I should have devoted more time to potentially more useful activities such as learning to pray

BUS. Tall red bus important as a symbol shit that guy again what's he got there

— We are now experiencing a small amount of

TUBE. The lights have gone they've gone where've the lights

BUS. What's he fiddling with his

PLANE. Did someone just go in the cockpit then a thud there was a thud

— 41 to

— Knightsbridge

BUS. What's he got

PLANE. And we're dropping now in my stomach

TUBE. Put the lights back on no please

PLANE. Gripping the armrests

BUS. Not with his rucksack he

— Mind the

— Hyde Park Corner

TUBE. Please lights lights

PLANE. Who's in the cockpit

BUS. Don't make eye contact but shit what's he fiddling shit don't shit

— Your attention please

PLANE. Still dropping dropping

BUS. Shit shit

— Piccadilly Circus

BUS. Shit no please

— Leicester Square

PLANE. Stomach jumped up into my

BUS. Close your eyes hold it hold it

— Covent Garden

PLANE. Jumped out of my

— Holborn

TUBE. Please

— Russell Square

PLANE. I

— King's Cross St Pancras

BUS. Shit fuck shit

Silence. Five seconds.

It's just his phone it's just his phone thank fuck it's just his

PLANE. A steward I think just a steward

TUBE. Back on again

BUS. I'll definitely have a nice warm bath as a reward when I get home

PLANE. God felt like for ever those seconds of drop

TUBE. But if I worry like this then they've won

PLANE. They've won if I worry like this

BUS. Then they've won if I worry like

— Where this train terminates

— The outside temperature is

— Now arriving at

— Connecting flights

TUBE. And it's funny and silly to say I know

PLANE. Almost disappointing in a way

BUS. I don't know why but I feel

PLANE. All worked up for nothing

TUBE. Like there was a part of me that even yes

ALL. Hoped that it was going to happen

PLANE. When you wait for the climax but the climax doesn't

TUBE. Hoping the thing you hoped so much would never happen would happen

BUS. Just for the hell of it

— We are now approaching

PLANE. Chance to impress the hostess as I leave

— A pleasant onbound

— Where this train terminates

TUBE. And it is the loneliest place in the world

— Where this train

— Step back to allow customers to exit

TUBE. And it disturbs me that it would take something like that to get us to talk to one another

— Please mind the

— Please ensure you have all personal items with you

— On behalf of the captain and the crew

TUBE. The loneliest place in the world

— We wish you a pleasant

— On behalf of

PLANE. Didn't even make eye contact

BUS. Can almost touch the bubbles

TUBE. The loneliest place in the world

PLANE. Maybe next time I'll smile at her at least

BUS. Just dip my toe in

TUBE. Until you arrive

— We wish you

TUBE. Until you arrive

— Until next time

TUBE. Until you arrive

— Until next time

— Where this train

— Have a nice

— Terminates

— Have a nice

— Terminates

— Have a nice

— Terminates

— Terminates

— Day

BLACK GIRL GONE

Janine Nabers

Characters

GIRL, *black*

WOMAN, *a minority as well. Older than expected*

MAN, *a doctor… of sorts. Minority if possible*

CHILD, *or an idea of one*

Stale harsh light illuminates a basement. A desk sits in front of a brick wall.

The glare of a TV can be seen. The glare hangs above the room like a sun of color. It is on mute.

A light from somewhere above buzzes lighting the face of the GIRL. *She is black and slightly tattered. She sits in a chair and clutches her book bag. She stares at the buzzing light almost in a trance... somewhere else even.*

She then sees a bowl of bright candy sitting in front of her. She takes a piece and eats it quickly. She's about to take another one when:

A WOMAN *enters and the door behind her shuts loudly.*

The GIRL *is slightly startled.*

The GIRL *and the* WOMAN *stare at each other.*

WOMAN. You the nine o'clock?

GIRL. Uh-huh.

WOMAN. You're early.

GIRL. I was hopin' you could see me now.

WOMAN. Doctor ain't ready yet.

GIRL. I gotta be somewhere.

The WOMAN *gives her a 'look'.*

I got class in Queens. At ten. I can't be late.

WOMAN. Financial District's a long way from Queens. You won't make it.

GIRL. A girl I know...

She said you do it really quick.

The WOMAN*'s look remains... unmoved.*

I don't need to be cared for afterwards. I don't need any special attention.

A moment.

WOMAN. How old are you, sweetheart?

GIRL. Old enough.

WOMAN. You got an ID?

GIRL. I got money.

A stare-off. This should take some time.

The WOMAN *picks up a clipboard and goes to the* GIRL.

The WOMAN *looks at the bowl of candy.*

WOMAN. You're not supposed to eat anything beforehand.

GIRL. I know. I'm sorry.

WOMAN. Don't worry. I won't tell anyone.

The WOMAN *hands the* GIRL *a clipboard and paper.*

Make sure you read *everything*. Date here signature here.

The GIRL *goes to write then stops.*

GIRL. I keep looking up.

WOMAN. What for?

GIRL. Don't know.

The WOMAN *hands the* GIRL *a pen.*

WOMAN. Just sign it. You're much better off this way.

The GIRL *takes the pen and signs.*

I'll be next to you the whole time.

The WOMAN *looks at the TV, which we do not see.*

The WOMAN *changes the channel with a remote.*

Click, click click...

News station after news station after news station...

Nothing interesting.

Look at this crap.

The GIRL *looks at the TV too.*

Don't know why I turn it on. Same pointless news every day.

GIRL. You want the money now or what?

WOMAN. We only take cash.

GIRL. I know.

*The GIRL hands the WOMAN an envelope. The WOMAN
counts the money and then goes to the door.*

WOMAN. I'll let him know you're here.

The WOMAN is almost gone:

GIRL. Wait, what's today's date?

The WOMAN shuts the door behind her.

The GIRL sucks her teeth.

*The GIRL starts to write but then stops. She puts her hand on her
stomach... after a moment she moves her hand.*

Stop bein' fuckin' stupid.

She signs the papers.

She waits.

She stares back at the buzzing light.

*The buzzing light begins to flicker first slowly and then fast.
Under the flickering light a small black CHILD appears. The
CHILD is looking at the GIRL.*

The GIRL walks towards the light when:

An intense slam is heard. It's so intense the GIRL jolts.

The lights go off and then come back on.

The TV we do not see now has a color-striped glow.

The CHILD is gone.

*A car alarm goes off. Followed by another and another can be
heard outside.*

The GIRL is looking at where the CHILD was.

The WOMAN rushes in.

WOMAN. Jesus.

GIRL. Did you see / that?

WOMAN. Are you alright?

GIRL. I think so.

A MAN, a doctor, enters.

WOMAN. What in the hell was that?

MAN. Who knows?

Hello.

GIRL. Hi.

The MAN steps aside for the GIRL to enter the other room.

MAN. The room's right through here.

The GIRL looks at the WOMAN and then walks past the MAN into the next room.

Another buzzing light illuminates a bare medical table with a thin paper robe next to it. Large metal stirrups stick out from the table.

On a different table a large number of invasive medical equipment can be seen. All large. All scary-looking. Another glow can be seen from a TV we do not see. It is also now color-striped.

Take off your clothes. Lie down on the table and we'll begin when you're ready.

Take your time.

The GIRL stares at the stirrups.

The MAN turns around and puts gloves on.

The GIRL undresses completely. She puts the thin paper robe on but it's too small to cover her entire body.

The GIRL lies down on the table. She puts her feet in the stirrups.

The MAN turns back around and spreads her legs even further apart.

He sits down in front of her open legs.

GIRL. Can you put something under me? The table's really cold. I can feel my bones against it.

MAN. Just breathe. This is just like any other procedure. It's like any other day.

GIRL. Is that woman gonna be in here with me?

MAN. She will as soon / as –

GIRL. I want her.

Please.

I want her here.

The MAN *goes to the door and opens it.*

The WOMAN *enters.*

The glow from the TV changes.

The WOMAN *looks at it.*

WOMAN. The news is back on. Want me to turn it off?

MAN. It's fine. I like it on.

The GIRL *and* WOMAN *look at the TV we do not see.*

The MAN *goes to the table of instruments and picks up a needle.*

I'm about to insert a needle into your arm. It's just a tiny prick.

GIRL. Can you hold my hand?

WOMAN. I'm right here…

GIRL. Where's your hand?

WOMAN. Talk to me. Tell me a story.

GIRL. Um. I don't / really…

WOMAN. Anything. Tell me something about you.

GIRL. I run. Sometimes. At school.

WOMAN. That's nice.

GIRL. Track. I run. I run hurd–

The MAN *puts the needle into the* GIRL.

The GIRL *winces with pain.*

WOMAN. Just breathe. Let it relax you. Close your eyes. Keep
talking to me.

GIRL. I run hurdles…

I can outrun all the other girls I know…

I'm…

I…

WOMAN. Just close your eyes.

The glow from the TV changes. The orange rays illuminate the room. An orange stormy haze.

The only person looking at the TV screen is the WOMAN.

MAN. You're going to feel something cold on the inside of you. It's just my two fingers. I need to get a sense of the size and position of your uterus.

Breathe in and out for me.

GIRL *breathes in and out.*

MAN. Good girl. One mor–

The WOMAN taps the MAN's shoulder. He looks up at the TV we don't see.

The MAN and WOMAN look at each other.

The MAN pulls out of the GIRL.

The GIRL opens her eyes.

GIRL. Why'd you stop?

The MAN and WOMAN talk quietly.

Is something wrong with me?

The WOMAN leaves out the door.

Where is she – ?

MAN. Don't move too much.

GIRL. But –

The GIRL looks up at the TV we don't see.

Why's the sky that color?

MAN. It'll be alright. Don't move.

I'll be back in a moment.

He too exits out the door. The GIRL tries to stand but she is too dizzy. She can't get up.

We hear another massive slam. A huge jolt onstage. The sound of the slam is more intense. Almost as if part of a building has fallen on top of the one we are seeing now.

The room shakes and the lights cut off completely.

Total darkness. The muffled sounds of people screaming outside are heard. Horns blaring, things slamming into each other. Total chaos.

Suddenly a single buzzing light from above (the one from before) is illuminated again and we see the GIRL *still in her stirrups. Passed out like she's dead.*

The CHILD *can now also be seen. The* CHILD *stares at the* GIRL.

The GIRL *suddenly gasps as if coming up for air underwater. She sees the* CHILD. *The* CHILD *runs.*

GIRL. Wait!

The GIRL *pulls herself up out of the stirrups and runs after the* CHILD.

The GIRL *pushes through the front door and it opens.*

The CHILD *stands out in the ashy rain… the sound of chaos surrounds the two of them as they stand in the middle of a blanket white stage.*

The sound of total chaos can be heard. It's so loud it's almost unbearable. People screaming, sirens blaring, things falling.

The WOMAN *appears. She calls from inside the clinic.*

She screams over the noise.

WOMAN. YOU NEED TO COME BACK INSIDE!

The GIRL *turns to look at the* CHILD *but the* CHILD *has now disappeared.*

YOU'RE SAFE IN HERE! IT'S OKAY! YOU DON'T NEED TO BE SCARED!

The GIRL *looks up into the sky, allowing the white to wash over her.*

The End.

THE ODDS

Lynn Nottage

182

Characters

ALI, *thirties, good-natured Yemenite*

AMEENA, *his wife*

DIONE, *thirties, a talkative African-American security guard*

EDDIE, *thirties, a jovial white guy in a business suit*

JOGGER, *thirties, a harried white woman in very skimpy running outfit*

A bodega. Boerum Hill, Brooklyn. 8 a.m.

Tuesday, September 11th, 2001.

ALI *stands behind the counter.* AMEENA, *in hijab, methodically sweeps the floor.* DIONE *enters, he grabs a carton of milk from the cooler.*

DIONE. What up, Ali?

ALI *(prounced 'Dye-own')*. Dione!!

DIONE. Tired as hell. Doing nights, trying to pull in some of that overtime – *(Sing-song.) Get it, spend it, money, money, money.* I'm looking to take my lady to the Bahamas in December.

ALI. Ahhh, the Ba-ha-mas.

DIONE. Yeah, the Bahamas, like, a real vacation.

ALI *(smiling)*. Don't talk to me about a vacation. I don't even understand this word, vacation. If I get to bed and to sleep at night this is my vacation.

ALI *laughs.*

DIONE. Well, I ain't cryin' for you, Ali. I know what you been up to. Ameena showed me a picture of the crib you're building in Yuh-man.

ALI *(proudly; correcting)*. Yemen. She showed you? Of course. I'm almost finished.

ALI *proudly displays a worn photograph of his dream house. He's shown the picture to everyone.*

DIONE. Now, that's the shit.

ALI. You like? Six bedrooms. I build slowly, five and half years. It would be quicker if I was there to supervise, but I'm always work… work, and everybody needs something. My son's at school in Sana'a, he needs a motorcycle. Why? Tell me why the boy can't take the bus like everyone else? AND! My mother, ay, she's sick, and doctors want to give her operation on her heart. It doesn't stop. Next year, I promised myself, no matter what, I'll see my house finished. *Inshallah,* but –

DIONE. That's how it is, man. Shit don't stop. Gimme three Newport loosies and yo Ali write down my numbers, 361, 268 and play today's date, what is it? Um, um –

ALI. The 11th.

DIONE. Yeah. Write 'em correct, cuz you always telling me I ain't hit. And I know I hit at least twice, and ain't get paid cuz you write that shit down wrong. WRONG!

ALI writes the numbers in a composition book.

Write it!

ALI. I write! I'm writing. Look, I write.

EDDIE enters.

EDDIE. Ali!

ALI. My friend.

EDDIE. Beautiful day? Huh?

ALI. No complaints here. Perfect day. You're up and out early.

EDDIE. Dog's walked, just dropped my kid off, first day of kindergarten.

ALI. Kindergarten? He's so big. I remember when he was like this high.

ALI measures the child from memory.

EDDIE. Yup. There were some tears, and then the little dude found a buddy and I was, like, history.

ALI. Egg sandwich?

EDDIE. Nah, not today. Lost fifteen pounds over the summer. Starting a new job.

DIONE. Looking good, you better go preach that sermon on the mount.

EDDIE. I'll take the news and a pack of lights.

A harried white woman JOGGER jogs in, past ALI, AMEENA, EDDIE and DIONE. She jogs in place, takes her pulse, digs into the freezer grabs a bottled water.

ALI. It looks like your team can't stay healthy.

EDDIE. Injuries all season. It's crunch time. But I'm keeping the faith. What's going on, Ali?

ALI. I have big big plans. It will surprise you. You'll see later today!

Suddenly –

AMEENA (*in Arabic; passionate*). Big plans? I'm so worried, where are we going to put everything? It cost more than it will give. Why couldn't we wait until next month for the delivery.

ALI (*in Arabic*). You are such a worrier, Ameena. You're going to give me a stroke. You complain, all of the time, when you should be working. Working harder!

DIONE, EDDIE *and the* JOGGER *watch* ALI *and his wife argue. It is a heated emotional battle.*

AMEENA (*in Arabic*). I work, I work some more and then I work again. Why do I have to do everything? Where's your brother Mohammed. He should be helping us. Where is Mohammed? Mohammed is out partying with his white prostitute girlfriend.

ALI (*in Arabic*). Enough with Mohammed. I ban you from saying his name.

AMEENA (*in Arabic*). Mohammed, Mohammed, Mohammed. I'll say his name, Mohammed if I want to. (*Shouts.*) Mohammed, Mohammed. Shame on your mother for naming such a lazy fool after the prophet.

The JOGGER, *thinking they're talking about her, self consciously adjusts her top. She's unnerved by the animated argument. She shoots* AMEENA *a dirty look.*

DIONE. Is everything okay?

ALI. It's okay. Okay. No problem. I am trying to make big things happen! This woman is scared of change. That's all.

AMEENA *sulks. The* JOGGER, *oozing condescension, throws money on the counter and rushes out.*

DIONE. And good morning to you!

ALI. Don't worry, she never speaks. Too important for us. It's these new folks.

EDDIE. Wall Street money.

DIONE. They know how to take shit from yo pocket without you even feeling it. They the niggers we need to be watching.

DIONE puts a carton of milk on the counter. He slaps money on the counter. ALI bags the milk.

Awright, my man. I'm outta here.

ALI. All right!

DIONE turns back, just before exiting.

DIONE. Ali, my numbers better hit. If they don't, I'm blaming you! It your fault. I better hit. I'll be back to collect my money.

ALI. *Inshallah.*

DIONE leaves. ALI and AMEENA go through the mundane dance of tending to the bodega.

A gust of smoke pours into the store, obscuring everything. A disembodied voice through the smoke.

RADIO DISPATCHER. You're at Two World Trade Center, the hundred-and-fifth floor. The fire department is on the scene... I understand that sir... They're on their way sir... They're trying to get up to you... I understand that. Try and stay calm.

The overwhelming sound of glass shattering.

Text projected on the smoke: 'Two days later'. Same. ALI and AMEENA in bodega. Smoke dissipates. AMEENA sweeps.

DIONE enters carrying an open carton of milk.

DIONE. Dang, it stank out there.

ALI. Tell me about it, my eyes sting from the smoke. Can you believe it? I still can't believe it.

DIONE. Nah, I can't believe it. I, like, got home just after I saw you man, and my moms calls, and she's, like, like, turn on the television. Man, dark crazy shit. Yo, I ran down to the promenade. And I saw the first building fall. Unbelievable. And... and the sky got dark and you couldn't see shit, it was snowing thick dust, like the grayest ugliest winter day. Man this shit weighs on my heart like nothing I ever known. Man, this shit makes me angry as hell. Like, like... I don't know.

ALI contemplates DIONE's words, and refrains from responding. DIONE places a carton of open milk on the counter.

ALI. What's this?

DIONE. The milk sour. Taste it and tell me it ain't sour.

ALI *smells the milk.*

ALI. Not sour! It's good.

DIONE. Don't smell it, taste it, taste it, nigga. That shit rancid, like it come out the ass of a dead cow. Your refrigerator ain't cold enough. Just gimme my money back! And we're square.

ALI. I put in a new refrigerator two days ago. It's cold. I can't help what happens to milk between when you leave my store and get home. Look at the date. The date says it's good, it's good. Blame the milk company, blame the refrigerator, blame the cow, but don't blame Ali.

DIONE. Oh, that's how it's gonna be. Awright, I'm gonna remember that next time when I walk a half-block to the Koreans and buy my muthafucking milk.

ALI. They'll charge you fifty cents more. And it will serve you right for trying to reach into my pocket.

DIONE. Man, you think I'm trying to get money off of you. I ain't a thief. You sold me sour milk.

A moment.

Dang, it still stank out there. Ya smell it? Bitter. Man, you seen it, the pile's smoking and it's as big as mountain. Like, I'm talking a real muthafucking mountain.

DIONE *is suddenly overwhelmed with emotions.*

Can't believe it. The wind keep blowin. Been blowing this a-way since yesterday. I wish it would change up, blow back toward Jersey. Man, it smell like death.

ALI *isn't smiling. He's sober, contemplative.*

Yo Ali, what happened to your window?

ALI. You see that! Some idiot threw a brick at it. A brick!

DIONE. That's fucked up.

ALI. It's fucked up! The police come, and they go like this.

ALI *raises his shoulders, 'Whaddaya want me to do?' gesture.*

What does that mean? I break your window, they put me in jail. Someone breaks my window and they go like this.

ALI *shrugs his shoulders again.*

You wanna see the brick?

AMEENA *shows him the brick.*

DIONE. Yeah man, that's a fucking brick.

ALI. A fucking brick. Can you believe it? The police tell me, it's not that kind of neighborhood. These people, they drink coffee that cost them $5, they want baguette not bread. I expect this from the niggers in the projects.

DIONE. Watch yourself! Niggas ain't a word you earned to right use.

ALI. I nigga, you nigga, we niggas. We niggas, that's what I mean. 'We' have to live with one brick in our hands.

DIONE. Awright. But watch that shit, you don't know how I live Ali.

ALI. This morning, I'm in the back, I hear glass breaking. I come out, and I see someone running away. And you can't believe who done it. It was that lady in the short jogging pants.

AMEENA *nods emphatically.*

DIONE. You know the one who always comes in here, her nose lifted so high she can't see nothing.

DIONE. Yup, she's like sexy, but… scary.

ALI. I run after her, she runs away. I'm running hard. *Inshallah.* But this woman, I don't know how, she runs faster. It's crazy. She's running like a speed demon, screaming and yelling all sorts of ugliness. 'Arab scum! Fuck you! Killers! Killers!' And the police see me chasing this white woman, and who do they stop? Ali. Fucking Ali.

DIONE. For real? That's fucked up.

ALI. I do business here for years. No complaints from anybody. The policeman… you know what he says to me, 'People are just letting off steam, gotta to have someone to shout at.' So they break my window? Because I am to blame for what has happened? They don't blame their government, they don't ask questions about why this happens. They don't ask where this anger comes from. They're idiots! Look, my heart hurts, the same as yours.

DIONE. But, man, that's how they do.

ALI. This is your country. You tell me why! Fucking speed-demon woman breaks my window with a brick, spews venom and they hold Ali for questioning.

AMEENA (*in Arabic*). Crazy woman!

DIONE. But, that was some ugly fucked up shit y'all done. Man, all them people. Man, it hurts. Man, I don't know. Whoa.

DIONE gets momentarily overwhelmed by the memory.

ALI. What do you mean 'we' done?

A moment.

DIONE. All you '*salaam alaikum*'-speaking dudes, you know. Allah make y'all do some crazy shit. You know what I'm talking about, Ali.

ALI. Oh, now you are throwing bricks? I better not know what you're talking about. This has nothing to do with Allah. 'We' don't do this.

DIONE. Yeah, yeah, tell it to them angry jihad-shouting motherfuckers. I think they beg to differ. All I'm saying is I understand why she did it, it don't make it right, but I know that kinda anger can make you do some evil dark shit. No offense, but if I'd seen you on Tuesday, I –

ALI. You'd what?!!

DIONE. I'm just saying. I'd have told you some shit. That's all.

ALI. This, what happened, has nothing to do with me. Understand. I have nothing to do with those people. Jihadist. Al-Qaeda. These are unreasonable people. Their ideology is as foreign to me as it is to you. That's the truth. I'm telling you the truth. Ask me when the last time I was at mosque. Ask me! Ask me! I don't understand this, they want life in… in… I don't want they want. What can I tell you?!

DIONE. I'm just saying. It's your people, man. I just don't understand.

ALI. Well, I don't understand your people. Okay.

DIONE. Whoa. You're stepping somewhere you better not go.

ALI. This is my store I can go where ever the fuck I want.

A moment.

DIONE. No disrespect, but you need to take two steps back!

EDDIE *enters, he's not his usual jovial self.*

ALI. Eddie, my man.

EDDIE (*tempered*). Hey, Ali.

EDDIE *doesn't meet* ALI's *eyes. He goes to the cooler and takes out a quart of orange juice and a carton of milk.*

ALI. Egg sandwich?

EDDIE. Not today.

ALI. You still on a diet?

EDDIE (*coldly*). Yeah… something like that.

DIONE. How ya doing, man?

EDDIE. Good. Still coping.

DIONE. Yeah, I feel ya.

EDDIE. I knew a guy from Cantor Fitzgerald, a buddy from college. Good dude.

ALI. I'm / sorry.

DIONE. Sorry, man.

EDDIE *says nothing, he cuts his eyes at* ALI, *as if to say 'I don't want your sympathy.' The air is heavy with sadness, tension.* EDDIE *takes his bag and leaves.*

You're gonna need a lot of window insurance. You got insurance?

ALI. I don't know. Basement floods, yes, store burns down, yes. Crazy speed-demon bitch throws a brick, I don't know.

AMEENA (*in Arabic*). What about the woman who broke the window?

ALI. She's asking me, 'What about the woman who broke the window?' You know what the cop tells me, 'We gotta lot we're dealing with right now. We lost a lot of our guys. Okay. Your window's broken, consider yourself fucking lucky. You have the precinct's number, call if you have any more trouble.' Any more trouble.

DIONE. Not surprised. I speak cop, and you know what he was saying, 'You're on your own, nigga.' They're finished. Done. They don't give... a... fuck. Been there.

A moment. ALI feels abandoned.

ALI. How can they treat me this way?

DIONE. How? You remember that little dude from the projects who you hauled off and smacked about a month ago.

ALI. Of course. He always comes in here and steals. Little thieving prick.

DIONE. And you know how you watch all the brothas like they done something wrong, right, cuz of that sneaky little thief.

ALI. They steal. I lose money every time they come in.

DIONE. You mean, he steals.

ALI. You have to watch all of them, who knows.

DIONE. You hear yourself?!

ALI. What?

DIONE. You hear yourself?

ALI. You're my friend, but... but that little one steals. I catch him every week. Potato chips, soda, he costs me money –

DIONE. How does it feel, nigga? Don't feel so good does it?

ALI. What are you talking about? Huh?

DIONE. What am I talking about? How you gonna feel when folks cross the street when they see you coming, how you gonna feel when they get off the subway when they see you and they wonder whether you that little thief trying to steal something from them. I tell you, they're gonna make you angry, cuz you know what they be thinking, even if it ain't true.

A moment.

ALI. ...I just run a grocery store, I don't ask for this. Have I ever done anything to you or anyone to deserve this?

DIONE. You sold me some sour milk!

ALI (*a flash of anger*). The milk wasn't sour when you bought it!!

DIONE. Yo, but it is now! That's what I'm telling you. And you still treating me like I'm trying to steal something from you, man.

A moment. ALI *goes into the cash register takes out some money and slams it on the counter.*

ALI. There!!

A moment. DIONE *scoops up the money.*

DIONE. And what about my number, it hit?

ALI. ... Not this time.

A moment.

DIONE. Put me down for 368, 361 and... 9... nah, that's it. You got it.

ALI. Writing. I write.

DIONE *starts to leave, then turns back.*

DIONE. Yo Ali, you know what my moms used to say, she'd rather keep her door open thinking the best of people, than always locked thinking the worse. I'm just saying. I don't wanna pay fifty cents more for milk. We cool?

ALI. ... We cool.

DIONE *leaves.* ALI *and* AMEENA *go about the running the bodega.*

not resentful at all

Harrison David Rivers

Characters

MAN, *twenty-nine*

A MAN *appears.*

The thing is
I was never overly concerned about it before

Beat.

It being my birthday

Beat.

I mean, I hadn't had a party since what, the fifth grade?
And I was fucking nineteen when it happened
So what, that's like eleven, twelve years of not caring...?

Beat.

And I mean, it wasn't like it changed my life
That like my life was ruined or whatever
It just

Beat.

(Sucked)

Beat.

And I get it, you know?
I get that it was this

He rephrases.

That it *is* this big thing
For a lot of people
And, you know, that there's no reason why

He rephrases, an attempt at diplomacy.

That people shouldn't be expected to like
Be *okay* or whatever

Beat.

To be able to like
I don't know

A gesture perhaps, a stand-in for words he can't seem to locate.

But

Beat.

Sometimes

Beat.

Okay
Full disclosure here

He takes a breath.

Sometimes I just want to be like
Fuck this
You know?
Fuck all of you
Because technically
It was my birthday before it was
This like
Global tragedy
So
I mean
You can at least like

Beat.

Acknowledge that.

He recovers.

But
I mean

Beat.

You can't say that to people
Because
Well

Beat.

Well
Because the undeniable fact is that
The joy or whatever of your birth twenty-nine years ago
My birth
On nine eleven eighty-one
Can't possibly compare to the general shittiness
Of nine eleven aught one.

End of play.

EPIC

Simon Schama

'So... how *Historic* is it, then?'

That's what they all kept on asking me ten years ago. Radio, papers, magazines; over and over. Especially calls from around here. 'Does it feel... really, truly... *Historic*?' 'Will we look back on it and say...?'

Well we are, aren't we? Isn't that why you're all here? Bald facts not enough for you not after all this time? Three thousand poor slobs minding their own business downtown, tapping away at their keyboards, waiting on tables; watching a ball game in the station house... smoked in the name of the Compassionate the All-Merciful? Need to dot a few i's and cross some t's?

What am I, some sort of magnitude-meter? Am I the one you want to pin an official certificate of enormity on the.... you know...?

Words. Are they up to it, I wonder? This one – enormity – no, class, not your synonym for... humungous – *Enormity:* something monstrous in scale *and* atrocious in wickedness.

Well, since you ask, I'd say it fits the bill wouldn't you? Bona fide Historical ENORMITY. Up there with the über-baddies: Sarajevo 1914, Black Death, Fall of Constantinople, assassination of Lincoln, Treblinka. You name them. Ticks all the Turning Point boxes... Life not same afterwards; never will be; fate of world irrevocably changed; beginning of the end of something (say, American solo superpower ascendancy), end of the beginning of something else (jihadi annihilations); turns out, gosh what a surprise, Professor Fukuyama a teensy bit premature declaring End of History; so yes again, this one, no question, supersize, jumbo-colossal mega-epic.

As urban bloodletting goes, yeah... really... fucking... epic.

Sorry. Wired a bit tight. Shouldn't sneer. Not if you're asking for official calamity certification from History Man. Better than the truism of the week, ten years ago... Remember how that one went? You heard it all over the place. People in far-flung parts – Alaska and Idaho and Paris and Hong Kong would come to wherever the local-news mic was and say... 'Wow, seeing the planes hit on TV, I

thought I was watching a disaster movie!' And just in case you
hadn't got it, the network would obligingly respool THAT video;
slo-mo nose cone, like some airborne shark, sticking itself through
steel and glass and out the other side as though it wanted to eat it;
the spray of lung-scouring dust; the livid blossom of flame. Super-
special FX!! The jihadis must have reckoned they needed a
Hollywood apocalypse, if it was going to register. Coming to a
screen near you. Atta-Boy Productions Presents the mother of all
blockbusters. Nothing left of the fucking block.

It needed to look *fake*, you see, before people could read it as *real*,
or as everyone likes to say now, as if real isn't enough, not for extra-
strength, added-value calamity… '*SURREAL*'.

You can't shake them off. Not again. 'But did you know *at the time*
how Historic it was?'

You mean, was I standing around *pondering* for posterity…
thinking, well this one's a dead cert for the history shelves at Barnes
and Noble? Trigger the creation of a thousand Departments of 9/11
Studies?

No not really. Like any other New Yorker that morning I was
keeping the panic at bay in one clenched fist while with the other
hand I was willing the dead cellphones back to life so I could find
out where my wife was on her Manhattan commute. I was doing a
deal with the God I didn't believe in to get her home. I was thinking
what I'd tell my son when I picked him up from school? What his
teachers had already said? Especially to the kids whose moms and
dads had set off for downtown that morning; thinking of any of them
we'd have to take in for the night.

What's that?… 'Just memories.' 'Not history.' Small potatoes; the
flotsam and jetsam of recollection. From me you're wanting the Big
Picture. MEANING. SIGNIFICANCE… An illumination? You want
the Take-Away from the disaster? God I hate that. Wisdom as
cheeseburger.

Look, what can I tell you? Sometimes the big picture *is* a just a
sticky little scrapbook of snapshots. Sometimes, memory has it all
over History for what actually matters. People remember. Professors
historicise. Mnemosyne's my girl, Goddess of Memory: pure
instinct. Nine hot nights on the couch with Zeus and bingo nine
Muses born, daily arrivals. Clio the Muse of History, always listed
first so has to be the Result from Monday don't you think? Top of
the class. Big sister to Terpsichore and the rest of the girls. Grew up

a bit Superior though, snooty even, embarrassed by Mum and her meandering recollections, always trawling through the trunk of souvenirs, rambling on. Dead soft that Mnemosyne. A bit dim as light bulbs go. Your Historical Muse, on the other hand, incandescent cool light, also a tough cookie, Miss Anna-Lytical.

If you really want to know the truth, bit of a cold-hearted bitch.

Still, you can understand her wanting the hand-wringing to stop; a moratorium on platitudes and pieties. Ten years. Enough already with the Bruce Springsteen Rising and the flags pinned to the radio antennae. Can we please let *thinking* begin. What was it Carlyle said about that other September massacre, Paris 1792; '*Beloved brother blockhead, well have ye shrieked at the horror, shriek ye but... acted have they...?*'

Lesson Time. What did we *learn*? Expressions of horror at the evil man can do, too banal? Time for a disquisition on the calculus of American power? On the socioeconomic contexts of jihadism? Time to put together cause and effect? Get the *perspective* that distance lends?

Well yes that's entirely reasonable. Trouble is, I'm not. I can't get the distance you see. Just don't have it. I put some space between now and then, a decade-shaped block of months and years. But it catches up in bad-dream time, invades my body space. I can still smell the bad breath of disaster on my face. There's some gritty deposit lying somewhere in my body the scan can't locate. The tarry bitterness wouldn't scrape off my pasty tongue not for years. And the odor; the fainter it got the more it hung around. How it smelled depended on the wind direction: metallic one day; rubbery the next. The smart on the cornea stung; the scratchy cinder you couldn't wipe from your eye; though you rubbed it red trying to get rid of the itch. The knot of yellow crud stayed in the gullet for weeks if you breathed in a bit of downtown. From the fourteenth-floor laboratory where my wife works you could see the ash plume hanging over the city as though someone had nailed it to the sky.

That sky. Everyone remembers. Merciless clarity. Azure hell. Not the pearly wet haze of high summer. Until it was fouled, this was the freshener; the back-to-school tonic; the September Invigorator. The blue out of which the bolt came.

Do you know, I heard it first on sports radio! Tuning in to baseball talk: pennant races, play-offs coming up – was the treat I'd given myself, for filing a piece a day ahead of deadline. Review of a show of early photographs of Egypt as it happens. Clever-clever stuff about the coinage of the word 'shot' for taking pictures; how the colonial lens 'took' the views, along with the stones, as spoils. Nice timing, right? Agonised discussions followed with the editor about whether or when we should run it at all during which, in about ten minutes I went from bone-headed affronted egomania ('of COURSE we should run it') to chastened self-effacement ('CAN it for God's sake; what was I *thinking*…?'). Editor agreed with position two. The baseball writers for whom a world crisis was a breakdown in the pitching rotation in the World Series didn't know what to say other than 'we're being attacked we're being attacked…' But what else *was* there to say…?

New Yorkers were knocked down along with the Towers; we stumbled along, on the edge of nausea; went a bit nuts; dropped things, broke things, lost things; drove too fast or too slow; hyperventilated, cried, prayed, yelled; smoked, drank; popped pills; over-caffeinated; crossed the street in the face of oncoming trucks, without caring until the blare of horns made us run; despite the nausea, headed for the cake; emptied the fridge drained the past-sell-by soured dregs; shoved handfuls of ice into our gobs, biting down on the cubes; hit the remote; never able to stand any one channel for more than seconds; took twenty-minute showers, so the drizzle of tears would wash away with the soap. We all tried to be practical for the kids. We couldn't do it and then we could because we had to. Between tendernesses we yelled at whomever was around. Had to do that too. The rest of the world doesn't get New York noise; the steam that gets let off from the street gratings or from the people who walk past them. It's nothing personal; just ventilation.

Disoriented is what we were, that endless Tuesday. Bearings lost. Phones not so smart then but they let us know where we all were and when. We were already mapped most minutes of the day. You could hear it on the trains. 'I'm HERE.' Where are 'YOU?' 'Oh you're THERE.' 'Well I'm HERE but I should be THERE. I'll call you… when I AM there.' But on 9/11 there was dead air and we were all at sea somewhere between here and there. Limbo. Purgatory. No Man's Land. Hilary, the pretty, dark-voiced woman who booked my book promotions, had an infant at day-care centre in the World Trade One. For nearly all of that endless Tuesday, she couldn't get near the place, nor in touch with anyone running the centre. All she saw was tumbling, self-pulverising ruin on the television. Only around sunset did the mum get her child back. The nanny who usually took her to One World Trade Center had shown up late… Didn't take her after all. But no way to let Hilary know.

The evening had us piece our stories together from broken fragments of communication. When she finally made it home late in the afternoon but my wife told me she had been turned back at a toll bridge entry to the city. It had taken the whole day to crawl the twenty-five miles home. Bridges and tunnels were being closed. As reports of rolling calamities came in – a second plane, Washington DC; Pennsylvania – nothing, especially not the girders of the mighty New York bridges, looked solid.

Was the city; the country going to hold? American parents were trying to protect their children from that sense of having the walls blown in by the wolf. Our teenagers were dealing it in their own ways; the older girl as is her habit thinking first of her college friends; worrying about any of them who had downtown working parents; the younger boy went very quiet.

His sixteenth birthday was coming up, nine days after the carnage. We'd promised him *The Producers*, the stage version. George Bush's way of striking back at terror – for the moment – was to get America to shop; but our way was to get to the theatre. Bialystock and Bloom. Just what the doctor ordered. Would the theatres even be open? Every kind of craziness was bowling through town: anthrax panics; dirty-bomb rumours…

But staunchness was forming; the speck of grit that seeds the black pearl. This was still Noo Yoik. The skull-gaunt whey-faced mayor we loved to hate, clambered through the broken girders and over the ash mounds; coughed with the firemen; did us all the favour of treating us like grown-ups; told the truth as best he knew it; left off politics for a bit to be a human.

No one was jumping town in terror but out in the suburbs there was a fair bit of lying low. Local trains rolled past melancholy with emptiness. Not us. We'd be staunch. They don't get US to slink away, no sir… 'Springtime for Hitler and Germaneee' we carolled in the car… 'Curtains for Po… land and France…' Out of the car we did our best to pretend midtown wasn't living through some sort of self-imposed semi-curfew. Tourists had fled once the airports had reopened. At our usual pre-theatre restaurant we had the waiters to ourselves. In Times Square, every spare surface: walls, storefronts, newspaper kiosks – was covered with photocopied faces of the missing. Tear-off phone numbers 'if you have seen' – Rhonda or Joey or Troy or Lisa – hung from the lamp posts like gray mourning weeds; ribbons of agony. A bunch of them had fallen to the pavement when the Scotch tape peeled away; so many they carpeted the sidewalk; a portrait gallery of New York faces; every race and complexion; age and build. So many that there was nothing for it to walk on their smiles. Even in the gutters you trod on the faces.

I hope to God one of them wasn't Laura.

I'm not saying anyone deserved what they got from the AttaBoys. I'm sure that among the multitudes of the murdered there were the fine and the good. But Laura? As far as I could see, she was nothing *but* good. She was the little sister to one of our best pals, Terry. But not much little about Laura. Very pretty, wide of face, large, dark, beautiful eyes; heart as big as a planet always it seemed to me, toting armfuls of children including ours; sticking spangles on their faces... feeding soft dough cookies into their crumby mouths; singing softly to them on wet November nights.

It was a stage family. Mother and father had been in New York theatre all their lives. So Laura was bound to be a trouper who nearly made it as actress. She ought to be here really to play herself. She managed a little Jewish rep company uptown; walked her dog in Riverside Park and to pay the rent she did the odd business seminar. In Windows on the World. So high up in World Trade Center One she couldn't have had a chance.

It took a long time to find out for sure. Too long on the rack for her family, her sister. There was, then, a memorial of terrible tears and brave smiles; where that dread phrase 'celebration of life' was uttered. Me? I'm all for an abyss of mourning. But you can't do that forever. It was what the sister, our friend did next that shook us... Wanting, even in the midst of all the raging misery, to turn it to something else. I told you. Impossible goodness runs in that family. So the only way Terry, the sister could make something decent out of the indecency, was to reach out to the Muslim world from which Laura's murderer's had come; to embrace their suffering too. Whenever she could speak against war, Terry did: Afghanistan, Iraq. Swords into ploughshares she thought; or somehow the hatred warriors would be victorious.

It was too much for me, I can tell you. We argued about it later, one night on the back deck of our house. I couldn't deal with Terry's saintliness; the cheek-turning. I wanted to stay with the rage; unforgiving; unforgetting.

I didn't mind the E-word on the mouth of the President at all. If 9/11 wasn't, cold-bloodedly, hot-bloodedly evil what was? And besides whatever other crimes and follies we might pin on George W. Bush, he managed one unequivocally good deed when it counted most: going to the Islamic Centre in Washington, nine days after the attacks, describing Islam as a religion of peace and saying as plainly as he could, that it was not the American way to demonise a whole faith for the crimes of their renegade sociopaths.

I don't see Dubya and Terry getting along. For Shock and Awe and the two wars she would, I think, abandon her peaceful sweetness and claw his face out. After trying to talk him round, of course. But the odd thing is that the Dubya of the mosque visit and the Terry of Peaceful Tomorrows – that's what she called the organisation of 9/11 families she founded – aren't that far apart.

I told you. You need the burn of memory to get to history. You need to take what happens to the heart into your head. Or else it's just PhD theses.

Here's what I think, a decade on from the end of Laura. We need to be militantly tolerant.

America once was; a piece of it anyway. The piece was Rhode Island where Roger Williams, founded Providence Plantation because he thought the Massachusetts Puritans had just imported Christian intolerance rather than forsworn it. The idea of the Plantation was that no sect could impose any views on anyone else; that sin should never be a crime; that no one could ever be held to account in a court for blasphemy; or anything else priests or imams or rabbis decided was intolerable. Nothing in the realm of beliefs *could* ever be held intolerable.

Not everyone went along with this in the 1600s, nor the 1700s. Rogue Island they called it through the Revolution. But there were Jews in Rogue Island. And not much later there was a Quran in the library of President Jefferson and in a peace treaty made with the Muslim states of the Maghreb, read by the first President, signed by the second and renewed by the third, an article spelled out that 'as the Government of the United States is not in any sense founded on the Christian religion… it has in itself no character of enmity against the laws, tranquillity and the religion of Mussulmen'.

Yeah that would go down like a dose of salts on the hustings wouldn't it? You're more likely to get the hue and cry – woe is us, for Sharia law is just around the corner in Nebraska. Punitive amputations are at hand in Oklahoma. Before you know it there will be stonings in Kentucky. Islamic Centre near Ground Zero?

Over our dead bodies.

Is that what we want, ten years on from the misery and the massacre? Hate for hate? War for war? Fanaticism for fanaticism? Body for body?

Two towers done, four more built in the same place. Higher and higher. Down they come. Up they go? The nah-nah-na-naah-naah school of town planning and architectural payback.

But maybe we need something bigger, taller, stronger.

Like an idea.

An Anglo-American idea. From the mouth and pen of Thomas Jefferson. Who got it from Locke. Who got it from Milton. Who could not imagine democracy without it.

Not an atheist among them. All three of them believers in a Creator. But who paid him the compliment of assuming since, as Jefferson put it, in his draft for the Virginia Statute of Religious Freedom 'Almighty God made the mind of man free', the most godlike quality invested in us is reason. Since the reasoning faculty was the kiss of godliness, matters of belief must never need anything but that faculty to sway us. The biggest affront we can commit to those beliefs is to imagine they ever need the help of the state. That there can ever be such a thing as a crime against religion. The more religion needs a police, the more it reveals its weakness, its falsehood.

And while I'm in the preachy mood let me just say that democracy is not in the piety business. It must tolerate everything but armed intolerance. Our only true enemies are the battalions of armed conformity. Jefferson said it best: 'it does no injury to me for my neighbour to say there are twenty gods or no god. It neither picks my pocket nor breaks my purse.'

Is the light of our Enlightenment so extinct that we have forgotten that this was supremely an *American* voice?

A voice that didn't shout 'GOD is great'.

What it said instead was

'Truth is great and will prevail if left to herself... she is the proper and sufficient antagonist to error and has nothing to fear from... conflict unless by human interposition disarmed of her natural weapons, free arguments and debate, errors ceasing to be dangerous when it is permitted freely to contradict them.'

That's what should rise from Ground Zero. In letters of light. Every night.

Because you don't measure victory by the height of the building, but the power of your idea.

You can't bomb an idea you see; you can't murder it, you can't cremate it.

The idea wins. The idea lives.

When it's the truth.

EVERYONE

Christopher Shinn

210

Characters

DR MILLER, *late forties/early fifties. Male or female*
STEPHEN, *late twenties/early thirties*

Setting

The play takes place now, in Manhattan, in an analyst's office.

Note on the Text

A pause does not necessarily indicate a length of time – I use it to convey that something non-verbal is happening within or between the characters. The pauses might be quite brief – it's really up to the actors and director as they work on the piece in rehearsal.

C. S.

DR MILLER *is on the phone.*

DR MILLER. I understand that, but you said this afternoon. Someone called an hour ago and told me – okay, but I need the car to drive home. I don't live in the city – I have to go. Please try to have the car ready by the end of the day.

DR MILLER *hangs up the phone. Goes to the door, opens it.*

STEPHEN *enters. He lies down on the couch.* DR MILLER *sits.*

STEPHEN. Well, I spent the weekend really trying to allow my feelings to – oh.

STEPHEN *sits up, picks up keys.*

Someone left their keys here.

DR MILLER. Must have been my last – thanks –

STEPHEN *hands over the keys.*

STEPHEN. Guess he'll come back in a minute –

DR MILLER. Depends when he realises –

STEPHEN. Right. I was in the waiting room when he left, seemed angry – the way he walked out –

STEPHEN *lies back down. Pause.*

Will you just – I guess you'll stop the session if he comes back to get them –

DR MILLER. It'll only take a second.

Pause.

What are your feelings about that?

STEPHEN. You know, you didn't need to actually say that.

Pause.

One day I'm gonna secretly film you so I can see if you ever at least smile at what I say.

Pause.

He did seem angry... The way he shut the door. Slammed it. I feel like I get angry but I don't go around slamming doors... But – I really want to focus on – I really felt more in touch over the weekend with – my anger, my rage, my longing for – I felt like – I didn't have to block out my feelings through masturbation or texting or Facebook –

A siren in the distance.

But it was hard. It kept building. The angrier I felt – I kept getting angrier – and I felt like – I was just trying to sit with my feelings and not flee them – read my book, do work around the apartment, but keep *feeling* – ... I feel like since coming here – I don't have random sex any more, I stopped being friends with people I don't really like, I cut out excessive drinking... I mean I want – I wanted a better life so – but we – or *I*, you never told me what to – I cut these things out and – now trying to cut out — stop looking at porn and jerking off or being on Facebook all the time – there's nothing to replace any of that stuff with, you know, and – so I'm left –

Siren fades.

– with all this – just – this *anger* – ...

At one point I went to look at porn to get away from it and – but I didn't really want to so it didn't really work when I – it could have – I could have made it work but I just – something – then I guess – I didn't know – I was agitated and – I got angry at *you*...

DR MILLER. When you say angry with me – what were your thoughts?

Pause.

STEPHEN. I think it scares me that we've been doing this for five years and only now am I... where was this anger before? I mean I know, it was in fucked-up relationships, excess drinking – but how could it have – I feel like that's just what most people *do* – it's how they, the people I know – but what I don't know is — now that I'm aware of it – what do I *do*...

Two sirens sound.

DR MILLER. – Those were your thoughts about *me*?

STEPHEN. No – I... I was – I guess this was Sunday afternoon, I was in bed reading... I thought about some people from my past, that I miss, people I've fallen out of touch with for whatever reason... then I started seeing your face suddenly...

DR MILLER. And...?

STEPHEN. Then... I just turned off.

DR MILLER. 'Turned off'?

STEPHEN. I don't mean sexually – and I know the fact that I just said 'I don't mean sexually' means I *did*, haha. But I mean... my... those thoughts I was having just turned off...

Sirens fade.

DR MILLER. So you saw my face and got angry and then... nothing?

Pause.

STEPHEN. – I pictured this couch. Being here. In the – during a regular – and I had a knife. And – I started – stabbing the couch and pulling out all the stuffing.

Pause.

And then – kept – when I reached the frame just – put my fist through it. And kept punching it and tearing strips of wood off –

Pause.

Then I ripped, broke the legs of the couch off and – started scraping the floor with them – slashing the – just stuffing everywhere and my hands all – gashed and bleeding...

Pause.

DR MILLER. And then?

STEPHEN. Then I started to jerk off. – Not here in the, in my – in reality. I pictured a webcam thing I'd, some guy I – but I couldn't.

DR MILLER. Couldn't...?

STEPHEN. – I kept closing down. Like a computer when you shut it down and it just – goes blank.

Pause.

DR MILLER. And then...?

STEPHEN. My hard-on went away. Then I had to meet a friend for dinner… By the time I got home it was getting late. I read a little, went to sleep. Woke up. Here I am.

Pause. Multiple sirens sound.

DR MILLER. What about now that you're here… try to go back to the place in your mind where you've destroyed the couch and see where your thoughts –

STEPHEN. I'm sorry – are you nervous? I'm officially nervous.

Pause.

The first two, okay, I thought – could be a fire. There were just a couple trucks. But this sounds like – four or five or – it sounds like multiple firehouses are being called and.

Pause.

I think something happened. I think – we should go online and look.

Pause.

I think there was an attack.

More sirens sound.

See? I think – I mean, this is not unusual to you or –

DR MILLER. I'm sorry, that last –

STEPHEN. THIS IS NOT UNUSUAL TO YOU? IT'S –

Pause.

I'M GOING TO LOOK ON MY PHONE.

Pause.

HOW CAN YOU NOT BE – ARE YOU – ARE YOU NOT –

Pause. Sirens fade.

How many trucks was that – …

What are you *thinking*?

Pause.

People go into – when 9/11 happened I got on the subway. *After* the second plane. I saw what happened, I was watching TV, and then I went about my day. It took me twenty minutes to realise that something had – that's why – denial is so easy to...

Pause.

You read about these people who escape serial killers – they followed their instinct, they knew something was wrong when they encountered them – another part of them said, oh, don't overreact, you're being silly – they didn't listen to that part and that's why they lived, their instinct enabled them to flee – ...

Pause.

DR MILLER. So am I the killer, or are you?

Which one of us is your instinct telling you to flee?

Pause.

STEPHEN. When you said could I go back... now that I'm here... and see where my thoughts...

I *can't*...

There's something stopping me – ...

DR MILLER. Something – or someone?

Pause.

STEPHEN. I feel like – if I felt it fully...

A knock at the door.

DR MILLER. I'm sorry – that's probably – just one second.

DR MILLER *goes to the door, opens it a bit, hands over keys. Returns.*

STEPHEN. Keys are about penetrating. You stick it in. Maybe he wants to stick it in you.

DR MILLER. Keys are also about opening.

STEPHEN. Or locking, don't forget that...

DR MILLER. So are you opening up? Or locking down?

Pause.

STEPHEN. I can't – it won't – how is this in me? How did I go so many years and it wasn't *in* me.

DR MILLER. It was in you, but you weren't aware of it.

STEPHEN. No! You don't *know* that! You can't just *say* that like it's a fact!

Pause. A siren sounds.

I hear that and my body tenses. I can't control it. It all *tenses*.

Pause. Siren fades. Phone rings. DR MILLER *silences it.*

DR MILLER. Sorry – ...

STEPHEN. Five years, that's never happened. Why – why did you leave your phone on?

Pause.

I want to stab the couch and rip the stuffing out... I want to punch the frame and tear it into pieces... I want to break the legs off and scrape your floor... I...

Pause.

Someday it's going to be what I thought it was. The sirens.

Pause.

Is this inside everybody? Is this inside you? Could *you* say it?

Can you say it for *me*?

What if he left his keys because...

DR MILLER. Because...?

Pause.

STEPHEN. I know there's a thought. I *know* it's there...

Everyone I know just lives...

Pause.

No. It's not gonna come. I'm sorry.

Silence.

Blank.

LYNNDIE ENGLAND

Beth Steel

Characters

DESIGNER, *Eddie, designer, twenty*

AGENT, *Roy, late fifties*

WRITER, *Gary, thirties*

LYNNDIE, *late twenties*

DESIGNER *is taking out his laptop and setting it up on a desk.*

AGENT. It comes down to gumption, hell our national narrative is about gumption.

DESIGNER. But is the plan to get a publisher further down the line?

WRITER. There's a lot of interest, for sure.

AGENT. Bottom line, we don't give a gnat's ass 'cause we have the gumption to do it out ourselves.

WRITER. It's proven difficult getting them to commit.

DESIGNER. Really? I mean, you know… she's famous.

WRITER. It's an important story and once people read it they will recognise that.

AGENT. Except for the spoilt Yalies who just love pissing on our fighting soldiers.

WRITER. But there's a renewed interest. I have no doubt that the book will do well. None.

Phone or door prompt.

That's her now.

WRITER *leaves.*

DESIGNER. Are you family?

AGENT. Press agent and friend.

DESIGNER. Right.

AGENT. Gulf War veteran.

DESIGNER. Would it be alright for me to have my picture with her?

AGENT. That depends on what you gonna do with it, boy.

DESIGNER. Nothing. Nothing, sir. I wasn't gonna ask her to, you know, do a Lynndie.

He demonstrates: hitch-hiking/rifle gesture, head tilted coolly back, a pen for a cigarette.

AGENT. The cigarette needs to hang a little lower.

DESIGNER. Right, right, you musta seen that a hundred times.

WRITER *and* LYNNDIE *enter.*

LYNNDIE. How you doing, Roy?

AGENT. Damn truck needs a new tire.

WRITER. This is Eddie.

DESIGNER (*raises hand*). Hi.

LYNNDIE (*nods*). Hi. You're a designer?

DESIGNER. Yeah. I stack product at Home Depot during the week. You're my first book design.

Beat.

I enjoyed your book.

LYNNDIE (*shrugs*). Gary's written it.

DESIGNER. Cigarette?

LYNNDIE. No thanks.

Beat.

DESIGNER. You sure?

LYNNDIE. I'm good.

Disappointed, he puts the packet away. WRITER *comes back over.*

WRITER. So, er, is it ready?

DESIGNER *is still staring at* LYNNDIE.

Eddie?

DESIGNER *looks at* WRITER.

Is it ready?

DESIGNER. Oh, er, yeah.

DESIGNER *sits down at the desk.*

Here it is. *Tortured.*

They gather round the screen. The image should be projected for the audience too.

So what do you think?

AGENT. What's not to like? Not a damned thing. (*Slaps the* DESIGNER.) Not a damned thing.

LYNNDIE. You never said you were using one a the pictures.

WRITER. Isn't it obvious?

LYNNDIE. So why did I do all them photos last month.

WRITER. We're using them too.

LYNNDIE. But that's the front cover there.

WRITER. Well, yeah, the photos will be on the inside.

LYNNDIE. But it's… (*Beat.*) This is where I get it wrong when I try and say what I think.

AGENT (*slaps* WRITER*'s back*). That's what Gary's here for.

WRITER. Think of it as turning a negative into positive.

AGENT (*agrees*). If you are doomed to eat shit you may as well bring your own fork.

They look at him.

Always been a maxim of mine.

LYNNDIE. Reason… reason I done this book is so that I can say more than this damn picture.

WRITER. And I'd hope that after eight months' work you can see that I've done that.

LYNNDIE. Right.

WRITER. But for people to hear that story, any of it, they need to buy the book first.

AGENT. Folks want to know what it is they're buying, from the soup to the nuts.

LYNNDIE. They'd be stupid if they dint – (*Snorts.*) says it right there: Lynndie England, Abu Ghraib –

WRITER. They know the face, not the name. The war, not the prison. It's been five years.

AGENT. But don't you worry soldier, I'm gonna work on your profile.

LYNNDIE (*quietly*). I got enough a one already.

WRITER. The point is, when people see this image they instantly remember.

DESIGNER. It's pretty iconic.

AGENT. Whole damn scandal.

WRITER. This *is* the war in Iraq.

Beat.

LYNNDIE. I'd like to try something else.

WRITER. I'm not sure what the problem is here?

AGENT. What d'you have in mind?

WRITER. It says 'Photographs That Shocked The World': we need that photo.

LYNNDIE. How about me now?

AGENT. A photo from now?

DESIGNER. That could shock.

WRITER. That's not going to work.

AGENT. Both pictures could be on there.

WRITER. There's only room for one.

DESIGNER. Lynndie now and Lynndie then?

AGENT. It'd be a compromise.

WRITER. This this is the picture.

AGENT (*points on screen*). If you just move her further on up…

DESIGNER. There'd be room for Lynndie now on the bottom…

AGENT. In a 'looking back over her shoulder' sort of pose…

DESIGNER. Hang on two secs, I just need to pull up the guy whose being Lynndied…

WRITER. We only need one Lynndie!

Pause.

AGENT. Well pardon me, buddy, but I think you need to calm down.

WRITER. I'm not excited, I'm frustrated.

AGENT. Excuse us for a moment.

WRITER. I have put myself on the fucking line here! You see that?

He points at the paper cup on the desk.

That's me right now.

All look at the desk.

DESIGNER. A paper cup?

WRITER. Used. Stained. Sucked dry. With teeth marks –

AGENT. Is this going anywhere?

WRITER. In the fucking bin.

He lobs the cup into the bin.

With my career. I was dropped by my agent today.

Beat.

She no longer wants to represent me.

DESIGNER. She didn't like the book?

WRITER. She'd seen the pictures, she wanted me to do it.

DESIGNER. That sucks.

WRITER. She said she'd forgotten what really happened. And now, having read it, she'd remembered.

DESIGNER. That really sucks.

WRITER. It's not the book she thought it was going to be.

LYNNDIE *shrugs indifferently.*

Nor are you the woman she had hoped you'd be.

LYNNDIE *smirks.*

You think that's funny?

LYNNDIE. The white trailer-trash gal. The low-ranking soldier. The bad apple.

They don't look at me and say this *is* the war in Iraq.

They say, this is not us.

LYNNDIE *lights a cigarette*.

I'm everything she hoped I'd be.

I'm anything.

Black.

MY NAME IS TANIA HEAD

Alexandra Wood

Characters

TANIA

I

TANIA.

My name is Tania Head.

I come from Spain, originally, but I've lived in New York for five years now, and I consider it my home. I do.

I'm glad to be here.

I'm glad to be here. That was something I learnt to say. When I did my course in Business English. I'm glad to be here. Insert at the start of presentation.

But when I say it today I mean it.

I am, truly, glad to be here, because I was on the seventy-eighth floor of the South Tower that day, and I could, very easily, have not been here now. I was one of only nineteen people above where the plane hit to survive.

I am glad to be here.

Although I'm only meeting you for the first time, you already feel like a kind of family. When I found your site and read what you've written about your experiences that day it was such a relief.

Shall I tell my story, is that something you –

She looks for affirmation from a member of the audience.

I should start with Dave. He was my fiancé and my best friend. We met when we both went for the same cab. I was in a rush, so was he, who isn't, so we shared it. And we shared almost everything else from then on. It was the first week that I was here. When I wrote and told my friends in Spain, I've met an American man, in a yellow cab, they thought I was joking. And I said, no, it happens! Even to someone like me. Dave was all-American, the athletic type, he played basketball in college, he was gorgeous. And he made me feel like the most beautiful woman on earth. So you can see how special he was.

He was killed in the North Tower, where he worked.

I was in the South Tower, as I said, on the seventy-eighth floor. When I looked around, just after it hit, it was like a horror movie. I was choking on the smell of burnt skin and people's insides. And I realised my right arm was on fire. It's funny, what came to me is what I learnt at school. I threw myself to the floor, and rolled to put it out.

She raises the right arm of her cardigan to reveal a scar.

The doctors have been wonderful.

In amongst all the chaos, all the screaming and the panic, I kept thinking about my white wedding dress, and swearing my love for Dave, we were supposed to get married that October, and I believe it was him, on his way to heaven, who led me out of there. I just kept thinking of our wedding day, and it kept me alive.

In Spain we have a saying, *a Dios rogando y con el mazo dando*. You have something similar, God helps those who help themselves. We should help each other. At the moment we have to stand outside the site with the tourists and the souvenir sellers. It's disgraceful. I would like to do what I can to secure access to Ground Zero, for those of us who feel it would help in the grieving process.

I worked for Merrill Lynch, that's what I was doing in the North Tower. I want to use whatever skills I have for, for good, I suppose.

We shouldn't be forgotten. I know I sound like a politician, and God knows we've had enough of them, but, I think it's very important.

We shouldn't be forgotten.

II

TANIA *catches a glimpse of a woman in a white wedding dress moving through a crowd (or the audience).*

III

TANIA.

I am glad to be here.

I am glad to be here.

I'm glad to be here today.

I'm glad to be here with you.

I'm very glad to be here.

I'm very glad to have been invited here today.

I'm glad to be able to speak to you today.

I'm glad to be able to speak to you.

I'm glad to be able to speak.

IV

TANIA.

I'm Tania Head, President of the WTC Survivors' Network, and I'm going to be

A camera flash.

your tour guide today. It's an honour to have been chosen to be your guide, Mayor Bloomberg, and I hope I can give you a true and straightforward account of how it was. I was in the South Tower and I lost my husband that day.

Oh, here?

She smiles for a camera. Flash.

I'd been at an eight-thirty meeting on the ninety-sixth floor. Those of us who were here always talk about how blue the sky was.

V

TANIA *catches another glimpse of the woman in the white wedding dress. The woman strides through the crowd, clearly looking for someone, and becoming increasingly panicked.*

VI

TANIA.

We, the survivors, shouldn't be forgotten.

We're not hawkers or tourists or parasites, we were there that day.

We have been forgotten.

I'm not a politician. I've met politicians. I'm no politician.

Before all this I would've been too shy to speak. To raise my hand. But why shouldn't I speak? Why shouldn't I raise my hand? No one's going to raise it for me. And why should I be afraid?

We survived and we should not be forgotten.

VII

TANIA.

It was luck that I read the article about him and his red bandanna. I thought you might like to meet someone he saved.

Your son was a hero and why shouldn't I tell you that? If anything I say is upsetting you of course just ask me to stop, but I can tell you about your son's last moments if you like, because I was there.

I worked for Deloitte, and I'd been at an eight-thirty meeting on the ninety-sixth floor. When the plane hit the North Tower we heard it, of course, and ran to the window. And already you could see people jumping. All I could think about was Dave, my husband, he worked in that tower.

I went to the Sky Lobby on the seventy-eighth floor to get an elevator and suddenly a plane tore through our building. I was knocked unconscious and when I woke up I was on fire, and a man, your son, was patting down my burning clothes and flesh. I couldn't really see his face, his red bandanna was over his nose and mouth, because of the smoke. But he was calm. If it hadn't been for him I'd be dead.

VIII

Audio clip from documentary footage of the 'real' Tania Head speaking.

TANIA.

I was in the South Tower and I lost my fiancé that day.

IX

TANIA.

I'm more than happy to talk to people about my experiences. I wouldn't be as involved as I am with the Survivors' Network if I wasn't happy.

I've spoken to Mayor Bloomberg for goodness' sake.

Yes his name was Dave, as I'm sure you know from any number of sources. I've done interviews before. There's nothing new to say.

Fighting over a cab, yes, it hasn't changed. And it's hardly going to now, is it.

I've spoken to the parents of Welles Crowther.

Why? Is there a job at the paper you have me in mind for?

Who did you say you were with?

I've spoken to one of your colleagues I'm sure. Don't you talk?

The usual way, why? T – A – N – I – A. Head. Can you spell that?

Giuliani. Pataki, for God's sake.

Have you actually spoken to any of the Survivors' Network? I was the one to get us access to Ground Zero, speak to them about that, about what that meant to them.

We do always talk about how blue the sky was.

I've organised meetings, lined up speakers, I found a specialist trauma expert to lead a couple of sessions. Ask them about that. Or are you only looking for holes?

How should I know, I was unconscious.

I am a survivor.

X

TANIA.

My name is Tania Head and on the fifth of February two thousand and eight I committed suicide.

Two days later, would they need longer to, no, one day later, on the sixth of February two thousand and eight an email appeared in the inboxes of various members of the WTC Survivors' Network informing them of my suicide.

I set fire to myself and went the way I should've gone.

I threw myself from a building. Like Dave did. Perhaps.

No, I set fire to myself. In the middle of a field, so no one.

They've stopped reading.

They think this is lies. Perhaps.

No details. Cleaner.

They've stopped reading because it's the end of the email.

Biographies

Samuel Adamson

Samuel Adamson's plays include *Southwark Fair*, *Mrs Affleck*, *Frank & Ferdinand* (National Theatre); *Boston Manor* (Theatre 503/Theatre Voice); *Fish and Company* (National Youth Theatre); *Clocks and Whistles* (Bush/Origin Theatre, NYC); *Drink, Dance, Laugh and Lie* (Bush/Channel 4); *Grace Note* (Peter Hall Company/Old Vic); *Some Kind of Bliss* (Trafalgar Studios/Brits Off Broadway, NYC); *Tomorrow Week* (Radio 3); *Breakfast at Tiffany's* (Theatre Royal Haymarket) and *All About My Mother* (Old Vic); as well as contributions to 24-Hour Plays (Old Vic) and *A Chain Play* (Almeida). His versions include *The Cherry Orchard* (Oxford Stage Company/Riverside Studios); *Three Sisters* (OSC tour/West End); *Pillars of the Community* (National Theatre); *A Doll's House* (Southwark Playhouse); *Professor Bernhardi* (Arcola/Radio 3) and *Transdanubia Dreaming* (National Theatre Studio). Film includes *Running for River*. He was Writer-in-Residence at the Bush Theatre in 1997–98, and his plays are published by Faber and Faber.

Mike Bartlett

Mike Bartlett's credits include, for Headlong, *Earthquakes in London*, which is about to embark on a UK tour. Other writing credits include *13* (National Theatre, October 2011); *Love, Love, Love* (Paines Plough); *Cock* (Royal Court; Olivier Award for Outstanding Achievement in an Affiliate Theatre); *Artefacts* (Bush; Old Vic New Voices Award) and *My Child* (Royal Court). Mike is currently Writer-in-Residence at the National Theatre and Associate Playwright at Paines Plough. In 2007 he was Pearson Playwright-in-Residence at the Royal Court. He won the Writer's Guild Tinniswood and Imison prizes for *Not Talking*, commissioned by BBC Radio 3.

Alecky Blythe

In 2003, Alecky Blythe set up Recorded Delivery (Verbatim Theatre Company) whose first production *Come Out Eli* at the Arcola, which transferred to BAC, won the Time Out Award for Best Production on the Fringe. *Strawberry Fields* for Pentabus, *I only Came Here for Six Months* with the British Council at KVS in Brussels, and *Cruising* at the Bush Theatre followed. In 2009 *The Girlfriend*

Experience transferred from the Royal Court to the Young Vic, and one of her most recent productions, *Do We Look Like Refugees?!* won a Fringe First Award at the Edinburgh Festival in 2010. Alecky's latest play, *London Road*, has successfully extended its run at the National Theatre.

Adam Brace

Adam Brace was born in London in 1980. He studied Writing for Performance (MA) at Goldsmiths. His first full-length play *Stovepipe* transferred to London in collaboration with the National Theatre and the Bush Theatre. Shorter plays include *A Real Humane Person Who Cares and All That* (Hill St, Edinburgh/Arcola) and *Midnight Your Time* (HighTide Festival/Assembly, Edinburgh). Adam also writes for and directs live comedy.

Ben Ellis

Ben Ellis' plays include *Unrestless* (Old Vic Coming Up Festival); *The Captive* (Finborough); *The Final Shot* (Theatre503); and *50 Ways to Leave Your Lover* (Bush/Latitude). He is well known in Australia for works including *Falling Petals* and *These People*. Ben has won the Patrick White Playwrights' Award, Wal Cherry Play of the Year, and was shortlisted in 2008 for the Bruntwood Prize. He is currently under commission to write a new work for over twenty graduating actors at Sydney's National Institute of Dramatic Arts (NIDA).

Ella Hickson

Ella Hickson is currently under commission to Headlong. Her debut play, *Eight*, won a Fringe First Award, the Carol Tambor Best of Edinburgh Award and was nominated for an Evening Standard Award. *Eight* went on to tour in New York and at Trafalgar Studios. Since then, Ella has also penned *Precious Little Talent* (Trafalgar Studios); *Soup* (Traverse); *Hot Mess* (Latitude/Arcola Tent) and *Boys*, and spent a year working with the Traverse Theatre as their Emerging Playwright-on-Attachment. She has taken part in the Royal Court Invitation Group and is a member of Old Vic New Voices. Ella is this year's Pearson Playwright-in-Residence at the Lyric, Hammersmith. For television and radio, Ella is under commission to Tiger Aspect and Carnival. Her Radio 4 play, *Rightfully Mine*, transmitted this year and her first short film, *Hold On Me*, has just been shot.

Samuel D. Hunter

Samuel D. Hunter's plays include *A Bright New Boise* (2011 OBIE Award for Playwriting and 2011 Drama Desk nomination for Best Play; upcoming production at Woolly Mammoth Theater Company

in Autumn 2011); *The Whale* (upcoming production at Denver
Center in Winter 2012); *Norway* (Phoenix Theatre of
Indianapolis/Boise Contemporary Theater); *Jack's Precious Moment*
(Page 73 Productions/59E59) and *Five Genocides* (Clubbed
Thumb/Ohio Theater). Internationally, his work has been translated
into Spanish and presented in Mexico City and Monterrey, and he
has worked in the West Bank with Ashtar Theatre of Ramallah and
Ayyam al-Masrah of Hebron. Awards include 2011 Sky Cooper
Prize, 2008–2009 PONY Fellowship and two Lincoln Center Le
Compte du Nuoy Awards. He holds degrees in playwriting from
NYU, the Iowa Playwrights Workshop, and Juilliard.

John Logan
John Logan received the Tony, Drama Desk, Outer Critics Circle
and Drama League Awards for his play *Red*. This play premiered at
the Donmar and at the Golden Theatre on Broadway. He is the
author of more than a dozen other plays including *Never the Sinner*
and *Hauptmann*. His work as a screenwriter includes *Rango*,
Coriolanus, *Sweeney Todd*, *The Aviator*, *Gladiator*, *The Last
Samurai*, *Any Given Sunday* and *RKO 281*.

Matthew Lopez
Matthew Lopez's play *The Whipping Man* has become one of the
more regularly produced new American plays in recent years. It was
seen in New York earlier this year at the Manhattan Theatre Club in
a production directed by Doug Hughes and starring Andre Braugher.
For this production, Matthew received the John Gassner Playwriting
Award by the New York Outer Critics Circle. Matthew's play
Somewhere is currently receiving its world premiere production at
The Old Globe in San Diego, directed by Giovanna Sardelli. He
holds new play commissions from Roundabout Theatre Company
and The Old Globe, where he is Artist-in-Residence. He is a New
York Theatre Workshop Usual Suspect and a recent member of the
Ars Nova Playgroup. Other plays include *Reverberation* and *Zoey's
Perfect Wedding*.

Mona Mansour
Mona Mansour's play *Urge for Going* was produced at the Public
Theater in April 2011. Previously, the play was read at The Public
(New Work Now), Golden Thread and the Ojai Playwrights
Conference. Mona completed a year in The Public's Emerging
Writers Group, where *The Hour of Feeling* was read in the Spotlight
Series. The play was also read at NY Stage and Film in July 2011.
Girl Scouts of America (co-written with Andrea Berloff) had

readings at New York Theatre Workshop, The Public (New Work Now) and a production in NYCFringe 2006. Television writing includes *Dead Like Me* and *Queens Supreme*. Current projects include a piece on journalist Anna Politkovskaya for Continuum Theater. Mona is most proud of having curated, with Lisa Kron, *Nuff Said*, a piece for gay, lesbian, and transgender youth that was performed at Dance Theater Workshop in NYC. She received an Honorable Mention for the Middle East America Playwright Award.

DC Moore
DC Moore's first full-length play *Alaska* was produced in 2007 at the Royal Court in the Jerwood Theatre Upstairs. In 2008, David was awarded the inaugural Tom Erhardt Bursary by the Peggy Ramsay Foundation which is given to support promising playwrights. Additional theatre credits include *The Empire* (Royal Court Jerwood Theatre Upstairs/Drum Theatre, Plymouth – TMA Award for Best Touring Production 2010, nominations for the Olivier Award for Achievement in an Affiliate Theatre and the Evening Standard Award for Most Promising Playwright, 2010); *Honest* (Northampton Theatres/Edinburgh Festival 2010); *Town* (Northampton Theatres) and *The Swan* (National Theatre). He is also the current Pearson Playwright-in-Residence at the Royal Court. For television, David's credits include *Jalalabad* (Great Meadow Productions/Channel 4) and *Home* (Channel 4's *Coming Up* at Edinburgh Film Festival, 2011).

Abi Morgan
Abi Morgan's plays include *Skinned* and *Sleeping Around* (Paines Plough); *Tiny Dynamite* (Traverse); *Tender* (Hampstead); *Splendour* (Fringe First Award at the Edinburgh Festival in 2000) and *Fugee* (National Theatre). Her television work includes *The Hour* (Kudos/BBC), *My Fragile Heart*, *Murder*, *Sex Traffic* (Channel 4), *Tsunami – The Aftermath*, *White Girl* and *Royal Wedding*. Her film-writing credits include *Brick Lane*, an adaptation of Monica Ali's bestseller. She also has a number of films in development including *The Invisible Woman* (BBC); *Suffragettes* (Film4, Focus and Ruby Films); *Little Mermaid* (Working Title) and her script *The Iron Lady* for DJ Films and Pathé is currently in post-production.

Rory Mullarkey
Rory Mullarkey is currently under commission to Headlong and the National Theatre. Rory graduated from Cambridge University in 2009 with a degree in Russian, Latin and Ukrainian, having spent most of 2008 living and working in Kyrgyzstan. Plays include

Single Sex (Royal Exchange, Manchester) and *Come to Where I'm From* (Paines Plough). In 2010, Rory was Writer-on-Attachment at the Royal Court and in 2011 he was made Pearson Playwright-in-Residence at the Royal Exchange, Manchester. Rory is also a translator of Russian drama, plays include *Remembrance Day* by Aleksejs Ščerbaks (Royal Court) and *Pagans* by Anna Yablonskaya (rehearsed reading, Royal Court). He has also translated plays for the ADC Theatre, Cambridge, the Free Theatre of Belarus and Radio Russia.

Janine Nabers

Janine Nabers is currently the P73 Playwriting Fellow (NYC). Her plays include *Annie Bosh is Missing* (2011 Sundance Theater Lab/Playwrights Horizons/Clubbed Thumb SuperLab); *Welcome to Jesus* (Soho Rep); *When the Levee Broke* (Workshop Theater Company); *Juniper, Jubilee* (Samuel French Festival Winner, 2008); *West of the Willow Tree* (2009 New Professional Theater Award and 2008 Princess Grace Finalist) and *Generation Graffiti* (Samuel French Festival Finalist, 2009). Janine is currently a member of MCC Playwrights' Coalition and the Dorothy Strelsin New American Writers' Group. She is an alumna of Ars Nova, Soho Rep Writer/Director Lab and The Dramatist Guild Playwriting Fellowship. Most recent work includes *We're Drunk/This is the End* (Old Vic New Voices); *A Beautiful Something* (music/lyrics by Sharon Kenny, book by Janine Nabers – Williamstown Theatre Festival). Janine currently has a commission from Playwrights Horizons in NYC. She holds an MFA in Playwriting from The New School for Drama and will be attending Juilliard as a playwriting fellow this autumn.

Lynn Nottage

Lynn Nottage's Pulitzer Prize-winning play *Ruined* has also received an OBIE, Lucille Lortel, New York Drama Critics' Circle, Drama Desk, and Outer Critics Circle Award for Best Play (Manhattan Theatre Club/Goodman Theatre). It premiered at the Almeida in April 2010 and is touring several US regional theatres in 2010–2011. Nottage is currently writing the screen adaptation for Oprah Winfrey's production company, Harpo Films and HBO. Other plays include *By The Way, Meet Vera Stark*; *Intimate Apparel* (New York Drama Critics' Circle Award for Best Play); *Fabulation, or the Re-Education of Undine* (OBIE Award); *Crumbs from the Table of Joy; Las Meninas; Mud, River, Stone; Por'knockers* and *POOF!* Nottage is the recipient of the 2010 Steinberg Distinguished Playwright Award, a MacArthur Foundation Genius Grant, the National Black

Theatre Festival's August Wilson Playwriting Award, the 2005
Guggenheim Grant for Playwriting, the 2004 PEN/Laura Pels Award
for Drama.

Harrison David Rivers

Harrison David Rivers' play *When Last We Flew* received the 2011
GLAAD Media Award for Outstanding Off Off Broadway Play and the
2010 Fringe NYC Excellence in Playwriting Award (2010 Sundance
Theater Lab/NYTW/Lincoln Center Directors' Lab/NYTW/Freedom
Train). Other plays include *Jack Perry is Alive (And Dating)*
(NYMF/Ars Nova); *look upon our lowliness* (The Movement Theater
Company); *lydie, or (s)he who looks inside, awakes* (Williamstown
Theatre Festival FreeWrite/New Dramatists); *the bandaged place*
(NYTW/Dartmouth); *And She Said, He Said, I Said Yes* (Joe's
Pub/HERE) and *we are misquoted texts, made right when you say us*
(Be Company/3LD Art & Technology Center). His short plays have
been produced at the Atlantic Theater, Atlantic Stage 2, Second Stage,
Joe's Pub and the American Airlines Theater on Broadway. Harrison
was a 2010–11 Van Lier Fellow (New Dramatists) and a 2009–10
Emerging Artist of Color Fellow (NYTW). He holds an MFA in
Playwriting from Columbia University.

Simon Schama

Simon Schama's theatre work includes a stage version of *Rough
Crossings* for Headlong, written by Caryl Phillips and directed by
Rupert Goold in 2007. He is Professor of Art History and History at
Columbia University, writer and broadcaster for the BBC and
Contributing Editor at the *Financial Times*. Simon's books include
Citizens: A Chronicle of the French Revolution, the *History of
Britain* trilogy, *The American Future: A History,* and *Scribble
Scribble Scribble*: *Writing on Ice Cream, Obama, Churchill and My
Mother*. His books have won the Wolfson Award for History, the
WH Smith Prize for Literature, the National Academy of Arts and
Letters Award for Literature and the National Book Critics' Circle
Award for Non-Fiction. His television work includes the award-
winning, Emmy-nominated *A History of Britain* and *Power of Art*
(2007 International Emmy Award for Best Arts Programme). His
forthcoming television project for BBC2 will air in spring 2012 as
part of the BBC's Shakespeare season.

Christopher Shinn

Christopher Shinn was born in Connecticut and currently lives in
New York. He is a winner of an OBIE in Playwriting and a
Guggenheim Fellowship. He was a finalist for the Pulitzer Prize in

Drama in 2008 and shortlisted for the Evening Standard Award for Best Play in 2009. His plays include *Four*, *Other People*, *The Coming World*, *What Didn't Happen*, *On the Mountain*, *Where Do We Live*, *Dying City*, *Now or Later* and *Picked*. His plays have been produced at the Royal Court, Lincoln Center Theater, Manhattan Theatre Club, the Vineyard Theatre, Playwrights Horizons, South Coast Rep and Soho Theatre, among others. His adaptation of *Hedda Gabler* for the Roundabout Theatre Company premiered on Broadway in 2009. He has received grants from the NEA/TCG Residency Program and the Peter S. Reed Foundation and he is recipient of the Robert S. Chesley Award. He teaches playwriting at the New School for Drama.

Beth Steel

Beth Steel was born in Nottingham and was part of the Invitation Group for Emerging Writers at the Royal Court and the writer's attachment programme 503/five at Theatre503. Her first full-length play, *Ditch*, opened at the HighTide festival 2010 and transferred to the Old Vic Tunnels.

Alexandra Wood

Alexandra Wood's play *The Eleventh Capital* was produced by the Royal Court as part of their Young Writers' Festival 2007, for which she won the George Devine Award for Most Promising Playwright. Other plays include *The Andes* (a finalist for the Susan Smith Blackburn Award 2011); *The Lion's Mouth* (part of Rough Cuts at the Royal Court); *Miles to Go* (Latitude Festival, 2008); *Unbroken* (The Gate); *Thirty Two Years is Nothing* and *Expecting* (BAC). She is currently under commission to the Young Vic and BBC Radio 4. In February 2012, the American Repertory Theatre, Boston, will produce Alexandra's adaptation of Jung Chang's *Wild Swans*.